Wilson's
Tales of the Borders

Revival Edition Volume 8

ISBN 978-1-913369-10-1

Published by the Wilson's Tales Project, 2021.

The authors assert their moral right to be identified as the originators of their work within the publication and retain their own copyright.

All rights reserved. No part of this publication may be reproduced, stored in a retrieval system or transmitted, in any form or by any means, electronic, mechanical, photocopying, recording or otherwise, without the prior permission of the contributors.

Design by Jon Goodyer

Edited by Joe Lang, Michael Scott-Watson, Richard Wilson and Nick Jones

Illustrated by Rebecca Douglas

Printed in Berwick-upon-Tweed by Martins the Printers Limited
www.martins-the-printers.com

Contents

Introduction
- *Foreword* 4
- *Wilson What was he like?* 7
- *Sacred Isabella* 12

The Rival Sheriffs of Teviotdale
- *The tale retold* 14
- *Background* 26

Rattling, Roaring Willie
- *The Tale retold* 30
- *Background* 45

The Monk of St Anthony
- *The Tale retold* 51
- *Background* 61

The Lost Heir of the House of Elphinstone
- *The Tale retold* 64
- *Background* 74

The Battle Of Dryffe Sands
- *The Tale retold* 80
- *Background* 91
- *Lord Maxwell's Goodnight* 98

Lord Kames's Puzzle
- *The Tale retold* 100
- *Background* 120

Small Tales
- *An Introduction* 124
- *The Vacant Chair* 125
- *Sunshine* 126
- *Something had to be done about it* 127
- *Untitled* 128
- *A Winning Yellow Piece of Pie* 129

A Foreword by Andrew Ayre

This eighth volume of our revival editions of Wilsons tales of the Borders brings a further selection of tales from Berwick and Scotland's Publishing sensation of the 19th century. Our enthusiastic team of writers, editors and researchers have distilled the tales into shorter and more readable contemporary language. Our researchers have looked behind the tales and characters to give them context and tell us which end of the "Historical, Traditionary and Imaginative" sub title they lie at. As always this gives a fascinating insight into the times, people, troubles, and challenges faced during the historic period of Border and Scottish history the tales cover. This edition includes tales covering a period of around 500 years for its source material.

Our biography of Wilson himself continues with a chapter on his character and personality in this edition.

We have again commissioned new illustrations to go with more traditional ones, portraits of some of the characters and photographs of places associated with the tales. Rebecca Douglas being our illustration artist this year, whilst Morag Eaton, whose work partly inspired the publication of our first edition, reflects on the inspiration she herself got from Wilson.

Our tale of The rival Sherriffs' takes us back to the time of chivalry and jousting. Dastardly dealing however plays as large a part as heroic acts as revenge is plotted. The two castles featured in this tale can still be visited and are well worth seeing, though very different experiences. The Hermitage is a desolate and foreboding ruin set in pretty much the middle of nowhere in the central Borders, whilst Dalhousie Castle is now a rather swish hotel just off the Edinburgh bypass.

Rattling, Roaring Willie one of my favourite tales sees a travelling minstrel ride a favourable wave of mistaken identity. The king who would be jester, has featured in previous tales and often chose to travel amongst his people as a Gaberlunzie, or travelling minstrel begging his way round the country offering his music and entertainment in return. No doubt also getting first hand intelligence on the state of the nation at grass root level in the process as well as some fun of his own.

In The monk of St Antony we also have a tale of disguise. However, this one leads to all sorts of difficulties rather than the quick and easy earner intended. The repentant impersonator complaining to his wife at the end that he had had "a bonny time aneuch to serve a man his hale life".

Both of these latter tales have been reproduced including a certain amount of "Scots dialect" in their narrative, which hopefully readers can more or less follow. 19th century readers were helped in this respect with the inclusion of a Glossary of the Scot's dialect at the end of the final volume.

The lost heir of Elphinstone, whist still quite a long tale even in its short form, is a real swashbuckling adventure of a tale. I like to think of it as a Pirate's of the Caribbean of its day. Even more so when I learnt in the companion piece that its author had a wooden leg, which was found to be full of Sovereign pieces on his death!

The Battle of Dryffe Sands heads for the more familiar territory of Border tales and ballads. Fierce and fatal clan rivalry. The battle of Dryffe sands was one of the last big inter clan battles. It involved some 2,500 to 3,000 people of whom about a third perished on the battlefield. The Johnstones were outnumbered but played a better tactical hand, including the technique which became known as the "Lockerbie lick". This involved seeking to slash your enemy, preferably across the face to the extent they became a blood casualty that took them and possible some others offering aid out of the battle, rather than getting bogged down in combat to the death. Disguise also plays its part in this tales jailbreaks.

Lord Kames puzzle comes from a series of tales, known as the "The Lawyers Tales" and is something of detectives tale as a girls true identity is sought with an ending twist to solve the conflicting evidence before the courts.

In recent years, we have also been including some new writing from the winners of our Schools writing competition, run in collaboration with Berwick Rotary and the Berwick Literary festival. Unfortunately, this became a Covid casualty this time round. In the last couple of years, the news has been full of daily reports of Covid cases and casualties. At the time of Wilson's death, the papers publishing his obituary were full of daily statistics of those dying from the Cholera outbreak that was rampant at that time. History does seem to repeat in similar ways.

We have however started a tradition of telling 100 word tales at our Wilson memorial dinner, a new tradition we have started to mark the anniversary of his death. The 100 word tale challenge being one originally set for Jeffrey Archer by the Readers Digest. The challenge being to craft a tale with a beginning, middle and end in exactly 100 words.

We will be sharing some of these with you.

Andrew Ayre

Wilson:

What was he Like?

What was Wilson like as a person? Whilst no Biographies were written during his life or at the time of his death, we do have a surprisingly rich selection of source documents to try to form an opinion of him as a person. We have his written works and even a selection of his letters written to his friend Everett, held at The National library of Scotland. We also have the benefit of various press articles on his activities and obituaries written at the time of his death.

Whist he came from very a modest background and suffered much hardship during his life, he was clearly hard working and ambitious and not afraid of taking risks and making his own luck as he had certainly not come from a family of privilege. He was also clearly a man of honour and principle.

His formal education was limited to what school in a market town could offer till he went to work, as he no doubt had to at age 11. He continued to self-educate himself from then onwards, there was no University opportunity beckoning for him. His first job was with a printing business where he is reported to have read what was being printed as part of his ongoing education. This would no doubt make for a rather random education and certainly not everyone's first published work at the age of 15 is a study of Hinduism! Over time he however became a writer of some talent and something of an expert on poetry, which he was to tour the country lecturing on as well as writing his own.

His formative years in Berwick were no doubt absorbing tales from a wide range of sources and we would be aware of the wider world from an early age. The Borders had a rich history of folklore and ballads, much of it giving a rather romanticised recollection of Border feuds and reiving. Berwick was also a major port. Sailor's yarns and experiences would also be an endless source of Tales. Much travel still happened by sea. Roads were poor and it was reckoned cheaper to get Wool to France by sea than to Glasgow by road. The journey to London on the speedy Berwick Smack sailing vessels took about a third of the time of a coach journey did and the fare included your food.

Merchant sailors, as well as ordinary citizens in the wrong place at the wrong time often found themselves press-ganged into naval service. Many sailors had fought in foreign wars, travelled to emerging empire and even been prisoners of war at some stage.

He seems to have had plenty of confidence, whether to set off to London to seek his fortune, promote his book, or to stand in front of audiences and talk at length on subjects from Temperance to Voting rights. At one point he contemplated immigrating to North America in search of better opportunity and before launching his own tales, had thought of taking over the struggling Kelso Chronicle.

As an editor, he seems to have taken a genuine interest in the issues and politics of the time. This included taking a clear position on issues of politics, most notably his support for the widening of the Vote through The Great Reform Act even if this meant going against the establishment and views of more established literary figures such as Sir Walter Scott. As such, I feel he had the sentiments of the common man and the Tales very much tell of people, places and lifestyles and events that most of his readers would be able to identify with.

He was a man of principle who felt his word and moral position were important. Shortly after accepting the position to come back to Berwick to be editor of the local paper, he was offered a similar role at The Manchester Chronicle, which later became today's Guardian paper. This would no doubt have been a more prestigious role and perhaps better paid, but he felt he had given his word to take up the post at Berwick, so turned it down. At the same time, he was also very anxious to ensure he had established his independence as an editor before accepting the Berwick roll. He wanted editorial freedom, not to be controlled by his employer.

He was a keen walker, both for pleasure, as we know of his walks up the Tweed as well as into the Cheviots. He also walked of necessity of circumstance. His wife and he having to walk most of the journey back to Berwick from London.

His wife was clearly supportive despite the difficulties they endured at times. His works and the tales generally have a feminist feel to them. Female characters feature frequently both as central heroines or the bed rock of families.

Wilson seems to have been a religious man, a member of the "Scotch" Church in Tweedmouth. He is known to have given speeches in support of the Temperance societies. He also had a lifelong friendship with James Everett, a Methodist preacher.

He was certainly hard working. He did not enjoy the best of health and it is perhaps overwork that contributed to his premature death at such a young age. It is hard to imagine the amount of work that must have been involved in the early days of his own self-publishing the tales. Not only continuing his "day job" as editor but writing the tales and organising the printing and distribution of the tales and all the commercial arrangements around this. Their popularity, growing circulation and demand for reprints would make this an even more complex and demanding task. One source also suggested he may have "over stimulated" himself in these exertions, perhaps code for a bit of helping opium consumption to keep himself going. Not an uncommon practice of creative types both then and now!

He seems to have been usually struggling for money and never really saw the success of the publications of the tales. Many of his descriptions of hunger and destitution are thought to be largely based on first-hand experience. On one of his early trips to London, he writes to his friend Everett that in making the arrangements;

> *"upon the cheapest calculation which I can make, I find it would require about two pounds more than I am in possession of. It is absolute agony for me to request you if you could befriend me with the loan of this sum…..I would have called on you, but I could not – it is with pain I have written this – and spoken it, I could not".*

The money was lent, as the trip to London happened, though not with the publishing success Wilson had hoped for. Latter correspondence apologises for the time he is taking to repay the loan. On one hand he later complains his employer has not yet paid him his annual salary, whilst elsewhere he reports of buying books at auction and building up his library.

Not that he often complained about his lack of money. Or his health. Rather he seemed to look for the positives in life. He wrote to Everett shortly after his arrival in Berwick. Whilst his health had not been good when he left Manchester, it got worse. However rather than describe and complain of his illness, he described his joy of recovery.

> *"When I again felt health in my veins and grasped in the pure air of heaven amidst my native fields, where larks poured down their tide of song, I seemed to swallow life, air, music and all! – everything teemed with delight.."*

As an orator, he seems to have been something of a showman. The Manchester Times & Gazette reported in April 1831 that; *"On first appearance of Mr Wilson, is that of a man of calm, thoughtful, unassuming modesty."* It goes on to say the tempo can quickly change and catch listeners by surprise. He *"convinces every listener both of his skill and of his power"*... *"his sudden transitions from the pathetic to the stern, the tragic to the comic, the rapid to the slow, the soft to the loud - accompanied by every variety of action, look and expression of feeling, can only be equalled by some of our best dramatic performers."*

He was clearly admired and respected by his peers and his death was widely reported in the national and regional press. Edinburgh's Caledonian Mercury reported he *"acquired a status in society... by dint of his own exertions and thus added another to the honourable examples of persons who have overcome difficulties and bettered their condition in the world. His efforts in the cause of reform will be remembered long."* As was his adoption and support of causes which identified with the liberties and comfort of the people.

His death was reported to the readers of the tales in the 49th edition of his tales in October 1835. Well worth a full read for those interested. As might be expected, it gives an interesting and generally supportive overview of his life. In particular it reported, *"He threw his whole soul into his work, and lent his unwearied efforts to promote what he considered* his "country's weal." *His spirit flashed with indignation at the thought either of public or private oppression, and he sought, with warmest zeal, to advance the interests of his native place."*

He was perhaps not without his critics. In Walter Scott's journals, he comments that he had heard from Wilson, who he clearly regarded as a little odious and had declined to meet him. Whether this was class snobbery or the fact they were at different sides of the political divide on voting reform, we do not know. Nor can we be sure it is the same Wilson of Border Tales fame. More locally, Mike Yates in his paper for the Music & Traditional music society tells of a local tradition that shortly after his burial an irate local woman flung an issue of the Tales on top of his grave shouting "*Here. Tak yer lees wi ye!*"

One gains the impression of Wilson as an intelligent, talented and ambitious man. Also a caring and thoughtful one, honourable in his wishes, hardworking and prepared to stand up for what he believed was correct rather than seek favour for personal benefit. He died at what seems a very young age to us, just as he reached success. Though at the time few in Europe lived beyond 40.

I often wonder what might have happened had he been of greater health and lived longer. The Tales under his sole authorship, rather than corrupted by poorer contributions of those who followed, might have launched a literary career to compare with Scott and Dickens, whose lives he straddled. Would he have turned his hand to politics and become one of the famous politicians of the Victoria era? He knew his time as editor at the Berwick Advertiser was probably drawing to a conclusion as the owner's son was returning from Edinburgh university and the expectation was he would be put in the position. Wilson would have had to find new pastures and take his career in a new direction.

We also have a good idea of what Wilson looked like as local artist and friend John Sinclair painted his portrait twice in the 1830's. One is with the Scottish National portrait gallery and the other is part of Berwick's own museum collection. Sketches based on these often appear as part of the frontispiece in latter editions of the Tales.

Andrew Ayre.

Sacred Isabella

"And the graves were opened; and many bodies of the saints which slept arose, and came out of the graves after his resurrection, and went into the holy city, and appeared unto many."

Matthew 52-53

'John Mackay Wilson and Sacred Isabella'. Paper-plate relief print on Fabriano paper

While working on the series "*The Red Hall or Berwick 1296*", I had a period of time where all creativity had deserted me. Wanting inspiration, I wandered over to the churchyard in Tweedmouth (the churchyard with its ornamented ancient graves is well-worth a detour) to look at John Mackay Wilson's grave for inspiration. It is a quite magnificent edifice, larger than I imagined and painted and peeling. As I walked around to get all the '*angles*', another gravestone superimposed itself in front of Wilson's. It said 'Sacred to the memory of Isabella'.

On one of the stairways in Tate Britain, there is Stanley Spencer's painting '*Resurrection, Cookham*'. At three metres by five and a half, it looks down on us and dominates the stairwell. It shows people emerging from their graves in Cookham churchyard to be greeted fondly by their friends and relatives. Spencer believed in a joyful day of resurrection. Everyone would be raised from the dead to receive judgement or glory irrespective of race. It was a belief I found intriguing. So here in a Tweedmouth churchyard in '*John Mackay Wilson and Sacred Isabella*', I '*resurrected*' both Wilson and Isabella to happily cavort in the land of the living. It has something of the air of a Donald Gill postcard and it is just a little bit '*saucy*'.

Morag Eaton

The Rival Sheriffs of Teviotdale

Context - Providence played its part in the early history of an independent and proud Scotland. The co-partnership of William Wallace and Robert the Bruce, triumphed over the insidious and cruel design of the English Kings. Soon, another two daring spirits, Sir William Douglas, the Knight of Liddesdale, and Sir Alexander Ramsay, of Dalhousie shone through that dark period of Scotland's oppression. This story tells of the fate of these two noble warriors.

Sir William Douglas - Sir William Douglas, commonly called the Knight of Liddesdale, was the natural son of Bruce's companion, Sir James Douglas, better known as 'Good Sir James'. Sir William inherited the military ardour, chivalric awareness, and domineering presence of his father. The Douglas lineage were remarkable for their height, gaunt-like expression and legendary strength. Their complexions were dark, and they acquired the designation of 'black'. Sir William was of a similar ilk to his father, and was instantly recognisable for his long, black curly hair, and despite a gashed, protruding lower jaw, he was regarded as extremely handsome by the ladies, and came to be known as 'The Flower of Chivalry'. It was as if he had been hewed out of the hard, dusky Scottish stone.

Sir William looked up to this father. The young knight, from his infancy, was trained in the art of war. The spirit of battle in the this young Scottish noble, was, not only a virtue, but a duty. He was never happier, than when in battle. He viewed it as a trade, and a service he owed to his country, suffering under the yolk of the English invader. This English hatred towards Scotland, produced in Sir William, an enthusiastic love of the military character, and a dogged patriotism. What contributed, however, most to the elevation of Sir William Douglas' character as a warrior, was the importance of chivalry.

No nation derived such important benefits from the institution of chivalry as Scotland. Excepting Bruce himself, Sir William had all the attributes of a true knight; his superiority of strength over almost every warrior, led him to behave in a manner that set him apart from all other knights. He readily attracted everyone's attention, their general respect, and their submission to his wily charms. Whenever and wherever, the Knight of Liddesdale appeared, the ladies' tokens of favour were unfurled, amid resounding cries of 'The Flower of Chivalry'.

Meantime, the gold of the English kings, had alienated the loyalty of many Scotsmen, who accepted money as an inducement. But not Sir William, he was incorruptible. He earned and acquired his title of "The Flower of the Chivalry', on his merits. But soon, hot on his heels, another bright star of knighthood, attained a place in that firmament too. The name of that other knight was Sir Alexander Ramsay of Dalhousie.

Sir Alexander Ramsay - Sir Alexander Ramsay, though but a young man, showed a wonderful aptitude for war, combining great bravery with an almost matchless ability to execute this gallantry in practice. In person, this distinguished captain was very unlike his contemporary and friend, the Knight of Liddesdale. He was of middle stature, but exceedingly strong, tough and hardy, and tireless, fleet of foot, and ever ready to put his plans into action. He could boast like Sir William, behaviours befitting those of a knight. He was handsome, with long auburn hair, with a personable and affable manner which served to win over the hearts of his countrymen and contemporaries.

What distinguished Ramsay most from the Knight of Liddesdale, was his integrity, evident no matter the circumstances, or situation he found himself in. Douglas, on the other hand, while deemed the perfect knight, kept up this appearance in public, but in his private life let his mantle fall, and behaved in ways in which even his own friends were uncomfortable. Ramsay, on the other hand, lived by the knight's code of honour, as imbued in him from an early age. In his private life, his honour was as dazzling, as on the field of battle or at the joust. His personal morals were held in high esteem by all, and rightly acquired the title of that of 'A Good Man'.

These are the two great captains who, in the minority of King David II, were called upon by the nation to save Scotland from the sword of King Edward III.

The Knights' Rivalry Surfaces

Long before Sir William Douglas 'The Flower of Chivalry' and, Sir Alexander Ramsay, 'A Good Man' came centre stage, to raise the hopes of Scotland, they had both separately been occupied in envisioning a plan of revenge against the sworn enemy. Both knights, responded to the call of their people to overturn the dismemberment of Scotland by Edward Balliol, whose treachery, by swearing fealty to Edward I, surrendered all Scotland's liberties.

Edward I, had twice, swept over the entire country, reeking death and destruction wherever he went. Scotland became a wasteland, princes of royal blood vacated their palaces, lords resigned their castles, and the ordinary folks gazed upon what remained of their homes that the English army destroyed. Fortunately, Scotland was afforded some respite with Edward making war with Philip of Valois on another front, leaving the Earl of Salisbury in charge. Scotland though bowed, was not beaten, and never regarded itself, a conquered people.

Together, Douglas and Ramsay, were the great knights of their time, they regularly trounced the English in battle. Their fame was widespread, and was shared equally. Their talents for waging and executing war comparable. Inevitably, a rivalry began to exist between them. Who should be the one honoured as the victor of a battle? Both men were different. Ramsay was generous in spirit in affording praise upon Douglas, but Douglas, could not bring it upon himself to share the plaudits with Sir Alexander. Neither with Ramsay, nor indeed anyone.

The Knight of Liddesdale was unable and unwilling to see any other Knight as his equal. He had earned that right, had he not? Douglas secretly, was annoyed with the fame of Ramsay. He became filled with envy, which degenerated into a genuine dislike for Ramsay, and anything 'Good' that was said about him. These feelings became magnified unfortunately, by a strange set of circumstances, not in any way of Ramsay's making.

The Reclaiming of Teviotdale and Hermitage Castle

The brave conduct of the two knights contributed to much of the expulsion of the English army from Scotland. The focus became Teviotdale, an area occupied by not only English soldiers, but English subjects too, who lived under the army's protection. They had ejected Scottish Lairds from their lands. Both knights, operating separately, but with the same aim, overpowered the English. Hermitage Castle fell to Douglas, but the prize of the wife of the English Lord Sir John Winton, Lady Winton, was appropriated by Ramsay, following his slaying of her husband.

By all accounts at the time, these captures ought to have been reversed. To Ramsay, the castle, and to Douglas, the beautiful Lady Winton.

Shortly afterwards, Ramsay offered to barter the Lady Winton to Douglas for Hermitage Castle, since his preference was the Castle. There ensued an unseemly exchange between the two knights. Douglas queried if the Lady Winton was worth of equal value to the Castle.

After all, he had not set eyes upon her, and accused Ramsay of talking up the value of Lady Winton, Ramsay's pawn in the proposed trade. Douglas laid out the problem. "My capture hath four wings (the castle), thine hath only two (the head and heart of Lady Winton).

Ramsay retorted, "I am unsure a castle can possibly have a head and a heart". "Thy comparison is too quaint for the purpose of trade", responded Douglas by explaining his castle was grounded, while Ramsay's Lady, was both mobile and autonomous. This suggested Lady Winton might choose to change her allegiance to Douglas. The undignified debate culminated in a request from Douglas. "Let us see the Lady, that we may not, as our townsmen say, make a blind bargain, and be only wise after the event".

This conversation, though intended by Ramsay as mere sport, disconcerted Douglas, who had no intention of giving up a castle, which he had wrung from English hands. He considered it unlikely Ramsay would indeed exchange Lady Winton for a castle. Douglas considered it not the character of a true knight that Ramsay hold Lady Winton against her wishes, as a bargaining tool, for a castle, or, as was suspected, to release a kinsman of Ramsay's who had been taken prisoner.

Ramsay spent the ensuing weeks doing everything in his power to inculcate Lady Winton into his life, introducing her to his friends, having her be part of his life. But Ramsay failed to understand that he could never eradicate from Lady Winton's mind, the fact that, by his own hand, Ramsay had taken from her the one true love of her life, her husband, Sir John. There was indeed nothing Ramsay could ever do, that would wash away the stain of blood from his hands.

Two Lords and the Lady Winton meet at Dalhousie

Soon after, Lady Winton was introduced to Douglas at Ramsay's residence, Dalhousie Castle. In the meantime, Ramsay had done what he could to make her as happy as was possible. The Lady Winton recognised immediately that in Douglas, was a person who might serve the purpose of her revenge on Ramsay. While Ramsay excused himself to take a message from the Earl of Moray, Douglas and Lady Winton had the opportunity of a few moments alone together. 'The Flower of Chivalry' took an instant liking to Lady Winton. They chanced to share each other's thoughts.

Sir William reminded Lady Winton, "The fortune of war has woefully changed thy condition, and it is the duty of us knights to protect the injured. I could be both your protector and comforter. What a pity that Ramsay killed your husband". Lady Winton quickly sensed the feelings and intention behind the remarks, and replied to Douglas, "If my husband was to fall, his fate came as well from Ramsay as from anyone. Nevertheless, I approve thy speech". Douglas smiled, well pleased that his hint, had placed Ramsay in an unfavourable light.

He went on to state, "thou hast done what in Scotland is deemed no trivial act, thou hast touched the heart of a Douglas, and enlisted his feelings of chivalry, in the cause of injured virtue".

Ramsay returned with a smile and some good news for Sir William. The Earl of Moray had bestowed upon Douglas the sheriffship of Liddesdale for expelling the English from that area. "And why", interrupted Douglas, irritated that it appeared the gift be as much Ramsay's patronage as the Earl's, "Why did the Earl who is nearby not communicate it to me himself, but vicariously". Sir Alexander was taken aback, and innocently explained the sequence of events, that he, Ramsay, had waived his privilege of the Governor's favour, and instead recommended that Sir William be given the sheriffship! The Earl requested that Ramsay, be the bearer of the news.

"The gift I receive," said Douglas doggedly; "but I admire neither the mode in which it has been conferred, nor the manner in which it has been communicated".

Douglas made it clear to Ramsay that everyone knew already that it was he, who had chased the English from Teviotdale, and was the obvious choice to be its sheriff. Lady Winton inflamed the situation by suggesting that Douglas might be now bound in gratitude to his benefactor Ramsay, by saying, "I have not witnessed such generosity of spirit across the whole of Scotland". Ramsay, was taken in by Lady Winton's false sentiments on this subject.

The meeting ended as Ramsay reminded Douglas of the upcoming jousting tournament at Berwick, telling him to bring a forgiving heart, and merciful hand. Ramsay added, "I hope Lady Winton shall be present to witness your triumph"?

The Great Jousting Tournament between Scotland and England at Berwick

Henry de Lancaster, Earl of Derby, knew of both Scottish knights' fame. As one of the best knights in the entire kingdom, Derby sought to test Douglas' and Ramsay's supposed accomplishment and prowess in a series of jousts. Three courses were to be run between Derby and Douglas; and then twenty English knights, led by Derby, were to compete with twenty Scottish knights, led by Ramsay. The scene was set for a trial of skill, between the greatest knights in the land, and two rival nations. It was attended by a great gathering.

An immense space of level ground was enclosed by palisades, and around the enclosure were placed seats for the spectators in the form of an amphitheatre. The ladies formed the most important personages as judges, as well as cheerleaders inciting the contestants. One of these was Lady Winton, who was dressed magnificently, and entranced many with her beauty. Sir William Douglas caught her eye, winning an enchanting smile, while Ramsay, instilled in her a shudder. The ensigns of war reminded Lady Winton all too well of the death of her husband. However, she maintained her composure and feigned a neutral position.

Derby entered the arena on his black charger, and challenged the Knight of Liddesdale on his white charger to the first joust. When Derby announced that his black steed's head would remain exposed, and not protected, so that his steed could see the discomfiture of his enemy, Douglas' blood rushed to his head uncontrollably. Losing his temper and presence of mind, he rushed at Derby, and was wounded severely by a splinter from his own lance, was unhorsed and at Derby's mercy. Ramsay ran to assist Douglas, who rebuked him. Douglas, wanted to fight on, but his hand had swollen so badly that he could not get it back into his glove, nor hold his lance. He had no choice but to exit the contest.

The Knight of Liddesdale, now bandaged up, retired to the seating area beside Lady Winton. She whispered in his ear, "Thou hast experienced for the second time the tender mercies of thy friend, Ramsay". Douglas retorted, "This man is indeed my evil genius". The tournament continued with the meeting of each set of twenty knights. After much fighting and bloodshed, Ramsay unhorsed the Earl with a side blow, sending him senseless to the ground. The judges awarded victory to the Scottish knights.

Lady Winton turned to Douglas, suggesting he had no option but to celebrate Ramsay's triumph. Douglas, could not bring himself to do this, and promptly began to exit for his castle at Hermitage. But before doing so, let slip, intentionally to Lady Winton, that Ramsay had wanted to exchange her for Hermitage Castle. "Heavens!" cried the Lady, "did the destroyer of my husband offer to sell me for an old house?" "He did," replied Douglas. Ramsay headed for the place where Douglas and Lady Winton had been sitting, only to find both had left. He was advised, that they had departed together for Hermitage Castle. The ingratitude of the lady, and the insulting behaviour of his fellow knight, piqued Ramsay's interest.

At Hermitage Castle

On arriving at the Castle, Douglas set apart for the lady a splendid suite of rooms. He hoped this would sweeten Lady Winton's nature towards him. But it seemed the harder he tried to impress the Lady Winton, the less Lady Winton approved. Douglas was now thinking she did not accompany him to the castle because of her affection for him perhaps, but solely for the purpose of getting away from Ramsay. Lady Winton had a clear motive for her actions. She sought revenge against the slayer of her husband but was scheming that the Knight of Liddesdale be the executor of her purpose.

It was plain to her that Douglas' feelings towards Ramsay, were the very reverse of those Ramsay held for Douglas. She could play on her affections for Douglas, while furthering her wicked purpose. The rival sheriff affair and the tournament outcome formed a good foundation for her plans. Resistance to Sir William was the first and most effectual part of her scheme. But she played him, and gently and slowly wound around her victim the chain by which she intended to lead him to ruin. She felt no affection for him really, and could never for a Scotsman. He was smitten.

Lady Winton reminded Douglas of the misconstrued acts of the generous Ramsay, which she knew angered Douglas. He could not cope with the notion of Ramsay's well-earned fame for the possession of noble qualities. He was satisfied, that although he excelled his rival in the daring dashing enterprises of border warfare, he was inferior to Ramsay in military art, in generosity, nobility of thought, conversation, beauty of sentiment and his fame in possessing these. But what galled Douglas the most was that whatever occurred, Ramsay always appeared to have, and assumed superiority over him.

Lady Winton was now content that Douglas could no longer let these matters rest. "What the heart wish, the judgment will not tarry to confirm, or the hand to execute", she thought to herself.

The Scheme/ The Sheriffship changes Hands

It now remained that this female schemer, bring about a train of circumstances. The die was cast. Lady Winton, through a close friend Clarissa Sofley, confidante of the Scottish Queen, learned that Ramsay was being talked of in high circles as the greatest of all the knights of Scotland, and a great favourite of the Queen. Lady Winton, of course, ensured Douglas was told about this. While Douglas rested at his Castle, Sir Alexander continued fighting the English, extracting them from Roxburgh Castle, by way of a daring night escapade, regarded as the most illustrious achievement of those times.

Sir William became even more envious of Ramsay when Lady Winton reported this to him. But Ramsay received not only praise for this daring deed, but a reward too. Lady Winton used her contacts and their influence to have it communicated at Scone Palace, that Douglas was tired of his role as Sheriff of Teviotdale, and that Ramsay's reward for the kindness he had shown her while she was his captive, might be the sheriffship. After all, and as part of the conspiracy, she inferred, this was what Ramsay had always wanted. So, both Lords would be satisfied with the outcome.

A few months later, King David conferred on Ramsay, for capturing Roxburgh Castle, the sheriffship of Teviotdale. Once more Lady Winton was able to report the news to Douglas but in a way that accentuated the gross injustice of the King's decision. Douglas effectively was dishonoured and disgraced by this announcement, and set himself on a course of revenge.

Ramsay's Rebuttal

Of course, Ramsay was surprised at the King's gift, since he had neither desired it, nor said anything to his King about the matter. He was intent on learning at first hand if it was true, that Douglas, no longer wanted to be Sheriff of Teviotdale. Ramsay delayed his acceptance of the King's gift, and rode with all speed to Hermitage Castle. Upon meeting Douglas, Ramsay said. "My king hath taken it into his royal head, that I am possessed of an especial desire to be sheriff. This cannot be so, since you fought so hard to win it. You should keep it."

Douglas responded, "By my faith Ramsay, thou art a right generous knight, and possess a miraculous power of producing opportunities to show forth thy noble sentiments. I received this sheriffship at your hands before, and I cannot prevail upon myself to tax thy generosity with a repetition of the same gift. Go sir, and take possession of thy sheriffship, and woe be tide you when you and your heirs issue edicts upon us Douglasses here in Teviotdale".

Douglas' Revenge

At this Douglas abruptly retired, leaving Ramsay aghast at his angry outburst. Ramsay returned to Dalhousie, fully resolved not to accept the sheriffship, and sent an intimation to that effect to the King at Scone. But meantime, Douglas refused to act as Sheriff, and the King required Ramsay to accept the sheriffship, and be invested with his new honours. It would seem that Ramsay might have expected some retaliation from Douglas because of this. But by simply resigning the sheriffship, Ramsay believed Douglas had now accepted the new situation. This was a pretence on Douglas' part.

Douglas, now intent upon the execution of his purpose, led a band of armed retainers to the church in Hawick, where the new sheriff was holding court. On entering, Ramsay signalled Douglas to take his seat alongside him. At that moment Douglas drew his sword, seized the victim, who was wounded in the attack, threw him with the help of his retainers, bleeding, over his horse and galloped to Hermitage Castle. Ramsay was thrown into a dungeon. Sir William allowed no one near Ramsay.

It was reported later that Douglas and Lady Winton sat outside the dungeon, to be regaled by the cries of a dying man. Harrowingly, Ramsay's agonies were extended, something that gave immense pleasure to his enemies. There was a granary above the dungeon, from which dripped, tortuous and slowly, particles of corn which found their way through the cracks in the floor. On these morsels Ramsay protracted a wretched existence for the space of seventeen days, until eventually hunger wrung from their victim the last spark of life.

Retold by Tony Douglas

The Rival Sheriffs companion piece

The Rival Sheriffs of Liddesdale takes place amid the Second Wars of Scottish Independence. Written in 1836 by an unknown successor to John Mackay Wilson, the author, like many a writer of work based on history, has played with the dates and the characters to forge a story. The 'romantic interest' injected by Lady Winton is probably completely fictitious. The background to the story is as follows.

The great hero, King Robert the Bruce had died in 1329 leaving the throne to his young son David II. In England, Bruce's adversary, Edward II had died two years previously. Edward's wife, Isabella had an affair with Roger Mortimer and they ruled as regents of England until Edward III turned 18 and gained authority, killing Mortimer and arresting his mother. During their disastrous tenure, Mortimer and Isabella had signed the Treaty of Northampton which was effectively a surrender to the Scots and entailed English nobility—thereafter known as the Disinherited—to give up their lands north of the border. The new King Edward made a priority of reversing this. The Disinherited launched an attack on the Scots in 1332 at Dupplin Moor, near Perth, in an attempt to replace the infant David with Edward Balliol, son of John Balliol whom Edward I had chosen as the 'puppet' king in 1292. Though victorious in battle the young pretender had to flee to England soon afterwards and Edward III responded at Halidon Hill outside Berwick a year later, humiliating the Scots. After Halidon, Edward turned his attention to the wars in France; Scotland was a battle he could do without. However, in December 1334, Edward marched on Roxburgh but achieved little, withdrew, and the following July returned with a much larger force and penetrated as far north as Aberdeen. One of his most trusted generals was Henry of Grosmont, 1st Duke of Lancaster (later Earl of Derby) who was put in charge of English-held Scotland until 1338.

There is some understandable confusion about one of the protagonists in the story. The trouble, as always, is that given names recur throughout the generations. Indeed, the official Douglas family website has two family trees with conflicting information. James 'The Good' Douglas, one of Bruces' great generals did have a son, William, Lord of Douglas, but William, 1st Earl of Douglas—the Knight of Liddesdale—seems to have been the son of Archibald Douglas, regent of Scotland and leader of the Scots army at Halidon Hill. He died there along with William, son of James.

Our William had been captured by the English earlier in 1333 and so escaped the carnage at Halidon. Thereafter, as Michael Brown puts it, 'The armed bands led by Douglas, his contemporary Alexander Ramsay and others lived "in poverty" and "like shadows", fighting a guerrilla war against the English… Ramsay based his followers in a network of caves at Hawthorndean in Midlothian, while Douglas, operated from lairs in the Ettrick Forest or the Pentland Hills…' Sir Alexander Ramsay of Dalhousie (just south of Edinburgh) was a notable warrior, made Warden of the Middle Marches, and famously relieved the siege of Dunbar Castle in 1338. That same year, Douglas captured Hermitage Castle.

In 1341, Stirling had been besieged by the Scots under the leadership of Douglas. Edward hastened to its rescue and arrived at Berwick on his way to the north, at the head of an army of 40,000 men and 6,000 horse. The news of the capitulation of Stirling garrison caused him to fall back upon Newcastle, and while he was there the Scots sent ambassadors to sue for peace. Edward, equally glad of a respite, granted a truce for six months. Immediately this was accomplished, the leaders of the different armies began to fraternise. Edward came and spent his Christmas at Roxburgh, which was still in his hands. Sir William Douglas visited the Earl of Derby, one of Edward's leaders, and was most hospitably received and entertained.

A centrepiece of The Rival Sheriffs is the jousting tournament. One of Edward III's strengths when first becoming king was recognising he needed the support of the nobility. He embraced and promoted the ideals of chivalry perhaps more than any monarch thus far. He modelled his court on that of King Arthur. His round table was the Order of the

Knights, a 'band of brothers' founded in 1344. To strengthen the bonds between fellow knights (and more importantly, to himself) he encouraged the joust, or tournay, an invaluable training method for many a young knight, despite resulting in injuries and deaths. For all that, there appear to have been strict controls and edicts were issued to prevent 'illegal' tournays around the country, lest they encourage rebellion.

The date of the tourney regaled in The Rival Sheriffs is debatable. The main history of Berwick available at the time of writing this tale would have been that by John Fuller in 1799. He writes:

> *In 1340, King Edward the III was at this place [Berwick] with an army of 40,000 foot and 6000 horse. Next year he celebrated the festival of Easter here, and held a tournament in which twelve Scottish Knights entered the lists with twelve of Edward's train. This spectacle was exhibited with that solemn pomp and great magnificence peculiar to those times; but, unfortunately, from the animosity which had long subsisted between the two nations, this mock-encounter was carried on with so much rancour and inveteracy, that two Scottish Knights were slain, as also Sir John Twiford, an English Knight.*

John Scott's mighty history of Berwick, written long after The Rival Sheriffs was created, quotes the chronicler Wyntoun (inspiration for the name Winton in the tale?) which might have been a source for our writer. In this account, Edward came to Berwick 'to spend the Easter of 1342 and jousting was engaged in with great zeal. Twelve Englishmen challenged twelve Scotch.' Wyntoun's account does match that in The Rival Sheriffs very closely.

The modern historian Peter Traquair reckons the first tournament between Douglas and Derby took place at Roxburgh in December 1341 and that the action then moved to Berwick in January for the second war tournament involving twenty knights including Ramsay. Ian Mortimer also places the joust at Roxburgh in December 1341, suggesting it was Douglas that approached Derby with a view, 'to joust for the prize of the Scottish castles which remained in English hands.'

Whatever the truth of the wheres and whens, the encounter did take place but these sources do not mention any animosity between Douglas and Ramsay. Maxwell attests to the rivalry between the two as often there was between noble houses in medieval England and Scotland. The flashpoint appears to have been Roxburgh castle. Perhaps in this episode we see something of the temper our author bestows upon Douglas. He was constable of Roxburgh and had failed more than once to seize it back from the English. In 1342 Ramsay succeeded in its capture and was was appointed constable of Roxburgh and Sheriff of Teviotdale. This, and the earlier success of Ramsay at the tournay, infuriated Douglas. As the tale concludes, Ramsay was set upon by Douglas and his men while holding court in Hawick and thrown in an oubliette at Hermitage to die of starvation after seventeen days. After intervention by the Stewart, Douglas was back in the King's favour and restored to his previous offices by late 1342.

Sources:

Brown, Michael: The Black Douglases, 1998

Fuller, Dr John: History of Berwick, 1799

Mortimer, Ian: The Perfect King; The Life of Edward III, 2006

Scott, John: Berwick-upon-Tweed: The History of the Town and Guild, 1888

Traquair, Peter: Freedom's Sword; Scotland's Wars of Independence, 1998

Rattling, Roaring Willie

You remember the King of the Commons, James V, the king who moved amongst his people? He could play and sing, but was no match for the Border Minstrel known as Rattling, Roaring Willie.

One day Willie decided to cross the Forth, and discover for himself the quality of Fife brewing. Taking his harp and a cudgel, he eventually found himself nearby the residence of the laird of Whinnyhill. With modest manner and quiet demeanour, quite different to his usual, he sought a night's quarters. The person at the gate was the laird himself.

"A night's quarters?" he queried, with a degree of respect which Willie couldn't understand. "That ye shall hae, sir, a score o' them if ye choose, the best that my puir house can afford." His look suggested more than Willie could comprehend, and he was conducted toward the best apartment. When Willie insisted on heading toward the kitchen the Laird whispered "Well, well, sir, ye will hae yer joke I see; but ye'll do me the honour to join me later when ye tire o' yer amusement."

Unable to comprehend this extraordinary kindness, Willie readily agreed. Domestic servants, eight or nine, lads and lassies, were in the kitchen. An audience for Willie. Ten minutes later the kitchen was an uproar of noise and laughter. He sang, danced, played, and pulled the girls about, till one and all declared they had never seen such a

harumscarum chiel in all their lives. His best stories were irresistible. Willie was triumphant as always. Amongst the merry minstrel's audience was the laird himself, showing a most unaccountable degree of respect for his guest. Willie was puzzled, even more confounded when the laird whispered, 'as they had now had plenty o' daffin, he would be glad of his company ben the hoose, where the guidwife had supper for them.'

In vain Willie said 'He wad just remain where he was, for he was not in the habit of sitting at gentlefolks' tables.' No excuses would avail. As his host would take no denial, Willie was soon seated at a plentiful board, with the 'guidwife' dressed in her best at the head.

Surprised though he was, his natural wit and confidence soon found himself perfectly at ease and joking with the laird and his wife till the roof rang again with laughter. After the bottle had made several rounds, Willie shone forth in truly meridian splendour. He broke out into the wild and obstreperous glee which characterised him in his cups. With the drink, and the excellent supper, he roared, and shouted, and sang, till the very rafters shook.

The laird and his lady were delighted, and he was no less pleased with them. When the lady retired, leaving her husband and Willie to finish the night and the bottle by themselves, cup followed cup as the bonds of friendship between them were drawn closer and closer. They grasped each other's hands in the fulness of their hearts, joining together in choruses of bacchanalian ditties which enlivened the festivity. However, the laird more than once hinted that he knew more of his guest than he was telling.

"However, I'm no one to spoil onybody's sport, much less yours. Only tak my advice, sir, and tak care o' yoursel, if ye be gaun through the Middlemass wood, for loose-looking characters were seen aboot there this last day."

"Ye ken mair o' me than I'm aware o', my honest friend," said Willie. "And as to the Middlemass wood, laird, I'll tak my chance wi' them. For I hae a bit airn here" clapping his hand on his sword, "that has stood me in guid stead mony a time before. I can tak or give, whenever such things are going."

"'Sir, ye play yer character to the life!" shouted the laird "Ye havna said or dune a thing the nicht oot o' joint, just as if ye had been at the trade a' yer life."

It was impossible their carouse could go on much longer and when they had finished every drop of drinkable liquor it came to a close. The laird conducted the minstrel to his sleeping apartment, where again Willie was surprised by finding that he had been shown to the best bedroom in the house. The sheets were white as a wreath of snow, the bed was of the softest down, altogether a complete contrast to the straw and ragged mats he was used to.

Willie flung himself into a chair, thinking over the events to see if there were any plausible account for the extraordinary hospitality. He thought up fancies with no sense, unable, to make anything of his conjecture, until he muttered 'I'm much obliged to him, at ony rate.' and he tumbled into bed. He had not lain more than a minute, when he heard a murmuring, from two persons in the adjoining apartment. The partition was only wood so he could hear everything spoken. The speakers were the laird and his wife. This is what he heard:

"But are ye sure it's him, John?" said Jenny.

"Sure that it's him!" replied the laird, "Nae doot o' that! Did ye ever ken me mista'en in my life when I said I was sure o' a thing? I knew him the moment I saw him, although I never saw him in my life before." He went on, "Onyone wi' a quick ee canna be mistaen. Besides, hadna I information, frae a quarter I couldna doot, that he had set oot on ane o' his vagaries, and there was every reason to believe that he had come oor way. And it's the very dress, too, that was described to me."

"It's a queer notion that o' the man's wanderin aboot the country this way," interrupted the laird's wife. "He maun meet wi' mony odd adventures when he's on thae tramps."

"His faither had the same trick before him," replied the laird, "I reckon it a lucky thing that he has come oor way. He'll no forget oor kindness, I dare say."

"And maybe he'll help us to oor ain again, frae the laird o' Haudthegrip."

"He's done the like afore. But mind we maunna let on that we ken wha he is; for he doesna like it. A' that I could say, could na drive him into a corner on that subject. Sae we maun tak nae mair notice o't; for ye ken kings are kittle cattle to deal wi'."

"So they're said to be, John," replied the laird's better half;"and I think the less we hae to do wi' them the better. This is the first night ever a king was under my roof, and I hope it'll be the last."

"Speak laigh, Jenny--speak laigh," the laird replied to the disloyal remark. "He's maybe no sleepin; and I wadna that he heard ye. For my part, I'm proud o' the honour. He's just as guid a fellow as ever I spent a nicht wi'. He tooms his bicker like a man, as your greybeard 'll witness in the mornin."

Willie was perplexed, then amazed when he heard all this, then realised why he was given the attention, kindness, and hospitality. There was no doubt he was mistaken for the king. James V. was in the habit of going about the country in disguise. Willie had also heard the king was a-roaming, here in the neighbourhood.

He was struck with the idea of maintaining the character to continue to enjoy the good living which was likely to accrue. He determined to be more dignified, be a little more guarded in his language, and, where he saw that he was not mistaken for a prince, to give hints to create the belief, or to confirm it. Having thought this out Willie fell to sleep, and in the morning, awoke a king in disguise.

Looking as majestic as he could when the laird enquired how he had slept, in a familiar but condescending manner, he saluted him with,

"Ha, laird! how dost? None the worse for thy potations last night? On my royal--ah! on my word, I mean--thou hast been nearer regicide than thou wotest of. Another such night and I would be a dead man!"

The laird, now fully believing that it was James standing before him produced a huge bottle of brandy which he had kept concealed behind his back, and filled up a large cup.

"Ye'll just tak a toothfu' o' this. It'll keep the cauld morning air aff yer stomach."

"Richt soond advice, laird," said Willie, draining the cup to the bottom, amazing the laird.

"Anither, sir?" said the latter, looking at him slily as he spoke.

"Why, laird, I don't mind if I do," replied Willie. He could not resist liquor, and he would have very soon forgotten his assumed dignity. Luckily the laird didn't press farther, and the danger was avoided.

His host now took Willie to a sumptuous breakfast, which he took with an appetite that gave his host a very high opinion of the state of his sovereign's health. Afterward ,Willie was asked,

"What direction do ye propose takin noo? I hear there's to be a gran' ball at Braehead tonicht. Ye might get some rare fun there, sir, just o' the kind ye like."

"Why, thank ye, Whinnyhill--thank ye for the hint! I'll just e'en go there, then. But what's the occasion, laird?"

"A hoose heatin sir. The laird o' Tumlinwa's takin possession o' his new hoose, and he's free wi' both meat an' drink. Ye'll want for naething, I'se warrant ye. But mind the Middlemass wood, sir, and keep a gleg ee about ye when ye're passin through 't; for as I was sayin before, there's some gay unchancy chiels thereabouts enow."

"Never fear me, laird," replied Willie; "I'll gie as guid's I get ony day--let who likes try 't."

Willie was ready to resume his journey, and at parting, Willie took his host by the hand, and with all the dignity he could muster, and a look which was intended to convey more than he could express, said,

"Fare-ye-well, laird, it may stand thee in good stead some day." And with this he walked off with as much majesty as he could assume, leaving the laird of Whinnyhill highly delighted with his opportunity of making the acquaintance and friendship of his sovereign.

Willie, in the meantime, after two or three hours walking, entered the wood and began keeping the sharp look-out recommended. So with wary steps he continued. About half way through, he perceived three or four suspicious-looking fellows skulking a little in advance of him, directly in his path.

'There they are! the very chiels the laird spoke aboot, or I'm greatly mistaen.' thought Willie, freeing his sword hilt ready for use. Although alarmed at the appalling odds, Willie held his course till within a few paces of the foremost, who stood with a drawn sword, masked and muffled in a cloak, as were all his companions. Willie also drew, demanding why he was being interrupted. No immediate reply came. The ruffians seemed doubtful, and Willie overheard them say as much. Besides, they seemed disconcerted by his resolute bearing and by his being armed. Thinking his assumed dignity might terrify them and save him from an unequal encounter, Willie called out, "What! would ye kill your King?"

"It is him! it is him!" they shouted "Down with the tyrant! Strike, Geordie, strike, for a thousand merks." They all rushed upon Willie. Willie instantly retreated. But it was not from fear. He retired in order to separate them, and having succeeded, he suddenly turned round, and before the nearest man was aware of his intention, ran him through. Having accomplished this, he continued his flight until another was considerably in advance of his companions, when he repeated the experiment. This time a desperate back blow on the pursuer's face inflicted a hideous wound that instantly disabled him. The other two lost heart and fled. But Willie's blood was up. He was both supple and dexterous, and overtaking the hindmost, ran the flying ruffian through the back, who fell dead. Thinking he had now done enough, and exhausted with the exertions, Willie allowed the last assailant to escape, then flung himself on the ground to recover breath, exclaiming, "Hech, but this has been a deevil o' a teuch job! This kingcraft 'ill never do. Here have I been as near murdered on account o't. I've nae notion o' the tred at a', wherr ye're cuttled up ae nicht, wi' the best to eat and drink, and next day to hae yer throat cut. It's no the thing, by ony means. The life o' a king is full o' peril."

Altogether, the experience decided him to resign the character, and all claims to its dignities. Then he decided to stick with it one day longer, until he had tried his treatment at Braehead. With this resolution, he started again, leaving the bodies where they had fallen.

Meantime, at Whinnyhill, another stout carle of a mendicant appeared. It was the dinner hour, so no egress or ingress was permitted till the meal concluded. The person though, began thundering at the gate, vehemently shouting at the top of his voice to open the gate to him.

The laird himself answered, more for the purpose of letting out his wrath on the noisy intruder, than to let him in.

"My feth, friend," he said, "An' ye had been the best man in the land, ye couldna hae been baulder. My certy, it's come to a pretty pass, when beggars bang at yer door like lords!"

"The devil's in the old churl!" replied the undaunted beggar. "Dost not see that I'm knocked up with fatigue, man, and didst think I was to stand here starving of hunger, if a few knocks at your gate was to bring me a little nearer to some refreshment? Come, Whinnyhill," he slapped him familiarly on the shoulder, continuing, "I know ye to be a good honest fellow, who grudges nobody either bite or sup. So let's have something to eat directly."

"By my feth, sirrah? but that's a new way to seek alms. If ye lack onything, it'll no be for want o' askin't."

"Why, Whinnyhill, a thing that's worth having is always worth asking."

"Ye're maybe no far wrang there, freend," said the laird, "but ye're ane o' the bauldest, ane o' the impudentest beggars I hae seen. Nevertheless, ye may step to the kitchen, for a mouthfu' o' what's gaun; but mind ye, dinna kick up such a stramash at my yett again, else I set the dog on ye."

The beggar, for answer, began a loud and gleeful song, which Whinnyhill impatiently broke into,

"Wow, man, but ye're as ill-mannered graceless loon as ever I saw atween the twa e'en. The greatest person in the land, is mair humble and respectfu' than you, when he's gaun about as ye're doin, and micht weel be an example to you and the like o' you."

"What mean ye, laird? of whom do ye speak?" said the beggar, disconcerted by the remark.

"I mean, sirrah, that the king himsel, when he ca's at ony decent man's house for a nicht's quarters, in his rambles, is far mair civil and discreet than ye are."

"Indeed, dost know the king personally, Whinny? Didst ever see him in the guise you mention?"

The laird grew angry, "Wad ye be the better if ye kent?" then in better humour, recollecting Willie's visit as something to boast of. "To be sure I do, sirrah! and weel I may, seein that he sleepit here a' last nicht, and's no three hours awa yet."

"What, Whinny! the king! The king here last night! Surely you are jesting, laird?"

"Jestin, sir! I'm nae jestin. The king was here last nicht, sirrah!"

"Impossible, Whinny!"

"Confound ye, sir!--wad ye make me a leear to my face?"

"Oh, no, no, laird," replied the other, laughing; "but you may be mistaken in your man. At any rate, if not impossible, it is certainly odd, Whinny."

"Odd, sir. What's odd about it? Do ye think the king wad think himsel demeaned by takin a nicht's quarters frae me?"

"Nay, nay; not at all, by no means laird, by no means. The man would be unworthy of being king who should think there was any degradation in sitting beneath the roof-and partaking of the hospitality of an honest and respectable man like you, Whinny. My surprise was at finding the king had been here, for I was informed he was in an entirely different part of the country. What like of a fellow was this king you speak of?"

"What like a fellow, sir! Fellow, in troth! Repeat that word again, sir, in thae disrespectfu' terms in the same breath wi' the king's name, and if I dinna teach ye better manners, blame me! Ye've muckle need o' a lesson, at ony rate."

"Very good, Whinny, very good," said the beggar, laughing heartily at the laird's angry earnestness. "I meant no offence, none whatever. I've as great a respect for the king as you can possibly have."

"It doesna look like it."

"But it is so, nevertheless, and I like you all the better for your loyalty."

"Ye like me a' the better! And wha the deil cares whether ye like me or no?"

"Well, well, Whinny," the beggar laughed, "But tell me how did you know the king in his disguise? Are ye sure it was him, after all?"

"Sure enough," said the laird gruffly; "he mair than half confessed it himsel."

"Oh, he did! then there can be no doubt of it, none. I should like to see his Majesty, laird. Can you tell me which way he has gone?"

"Ye're very inquisitive. The king's awa to Braehead, and that's the last ye'll hae frae me, sae get a mouthfu', and then tak yersel aff as sune's ye like." The laird was about to walk off, when the mendicant called him back, saying,

"Laird, canst keep a secret?"

"If it's worth keepin, maybe I can."

"Well then, I'm not altogether reconciled to dining in your kitchen, though I am particularly hungry; and therefore ask you what would you think if I was the king and that person, whom you took to be the king, was an impostor?"

"Wow, man, but that's a clumsy trick, I'm owre far north, lad, to be come owre that way."

"Well, laird," he smiled, "I assure you your penetration is at fault, for I tell you I am the king."

"And I tell you," replied the laird, "that I dinna believe a word o't; and mair, for your impudence in attempting to impose upon me, ye shanna get bite or sup here this day. Tak my word for that."

It was useless for James to try and pacify the laird, to convince him that he was the king, or even to let him have the refreshment he so much needed. Whinnyhill, obstinate at all times, was particularly so now, and the good-humoured monarch could say nothing to gain admittance, or the slightest hospitality.

James at length gave it up as hopeless; but though disappointed, fatigued and hungry, he saw that his churlish treatment came from the laird's love and respect for himself. He was greatly puzzled over who could possibly have taken up his identity; some one had done so for sure, and seemed successful in using it. The trick was a new one to him, and he was tickled by the ingenuity of someone using so novel an idea. His curiosity to see his rival was so great that he set out immediately for Braehead, about six or seven miles away, following his counterpart.

Middlemass wood was the direct and shortest route to the place, so the king's attention was soon arrested by the bodies which Willie had left behind.

King James stooped over the dying man, inquiring who he was, and what was the meaning of the horrid scene around him. The mutilated wretch fixed his almost sightless eyes on the face of the king,"I am a dying man, stranger; but I deserve my fate."

"Indeed!" said James, "What hand dealt thee that cruel blow?"

"The king's."

"The king's! what mean ye?"

"I mean that it was the king's sword that did this. We waylaid him, expecting he would come this way in disguise; but he was too many for us."

"And what motive had you for attacking the king?"

"We were hired."

"Ha! hired!" exclaimed James, in alarm! "who hired you? Speak, speak, man, who hired you?"

"I'll not tell," replied the man; "for I'm obliged to him. But stranger," he continued, "as you would have the blessings of a dying man upon your head, you will - you will," after a short interval he gasped "go to Falkland, and tell the king - the king - to beware of - of - "

"Whom, whom, man?" James interrupted, breathless with intense interest. The dying man slowly added, "Of the Earl of Bothwell" and expired.

"Ha! Bothwell! Bothwell!" repeated James, now falling into a profound reverie; "ay, is he at these pranks? I'll see him taken care of to play no more of them. It seems my counterpart has done me good service. I must have been slain by these ruffians. I'll forgive the dog his impudence, after all. Nay, he deserves a reward, and he shall have it too." Having thought this, James resumed his journey. Little more than an hour more brought James to Braehead. He entered the house, full of mirth and festivity from end to end, and uninvited and unopposed, walked into the kitchen.

The king was instantly attracted by a conspicuous figure at the farther end, enviably placed between two uncommonly pretty girls, whom he was entertaining with a noisy glee that afforded them great delight. But his exuberant spirit was not confined to his two fair supporters. He was in undisputed possession, there was no doubt he was first fiddle of the evening.

James at once guessed that he was the person who had represented him at Whinnyhill. Satisfied of this, the disguised monarch stole to where Willie was seated, and whispered in his ear,

"I say, friend, who the devil are you?"

"And I say," exclaimed Willie, looking hard at the enquirer "Wha the deevil are ye?"

"Just what you see me, going about the country seeking a living wherever I may pick it up."

"Nae harm in that ava, freen," said Willie. "Puir bodies maun live some way or anither. They're no gaun to die at a dike side if they can get a mouthfu' for the askin."

"Surely not, surely not, friend." Drawing Willie close to him, so as to be inaudible he added, "But, do you think I don't know you, sir, notwithstanding your disguise? I know you well, sir. You are the king!"

"And what though I be, sir?" said Willie, surprised to find royalty thrust upon him again. "What's that to you? But as ye value yer head, mum's the word aboot that, for I'm in very guid quarters and hae nae wish to gang amang the gentry."

"Nay, nay, I cannot stand to see my sovereign in such a humble situation. It is unseemly and painful to behold. I insist that you be treated with more respect. I must inform the laird of your being here." Without waiting, the monarch hurried out, desiring a servant to bring his master to the front of the house.

James then awaited the laird's appearance.

"Well, laird," said the King, "dost know me? I think you do. We have seen each other before."

The laird looked perplexedly at the disguised monarch. Finally doffing his bonnet with the most profound respect.

"I do, sir, I do. You are the king!"

"Hush, hush. Not a word of that just now. My crown's in danger, laird. There's a rival near my throne. Dost know there's another king in your kitchen at this moment?"

"You are pleased to be merry, sire. Pray, what does your Majesty mean?" replied the laird, smiling, yet at a loss to comprehend the joke.

"Why, I mean there is another king in your kitchen just now; a rattling, stalwart fellow with a couple of very pretty girls beside him. But, laird, the fellow in your kitchen has assumed my personage. He has already imposed upon Whinnyhill."

"The knave! We must have him instantly hanged."

"Nay, nay, not so fast. The fellow deserves a fright, and shall have it; but he has done me good service, though unwittingly, and I must forgive him." James related his experience in Middlemass, then he said, "Now, laird, we shall amuse ourselves. You wait on him, pretending to take him for the king. Insist on him joining you and your friends at your table. I think he'll flinch it if he can. A messenger shall announce my arrival, and then we shall sport with the rogue."

The laird, a bit of a joker himself, walked up, hat in hand, to Willie, and respectfully informed him that he had come to insist his guest accompanied him to a place more befitting his dignity.

"Why, laird," replied Willie, in his best manner, "I thank ye; but I'd rather remain where I am. I'm amazingly well here, and cannot think of leaving these twa bonny lasses."

"Nay, excuse me," said the laird, bowing low; "but I must insist. I will explain myself farther in a more fitting place."

"Why, if you so insist, laird, I do not see that I can refuse." With reluctance, he followed to an apartment where people were assembled round a well-stored table. Willie resolved to brave it out.

On his entrance, the party rose to their feet respectfully till Willie was at the head of the table. Every respect and attention which could have been bestowed upon the real king was granted Willie, excepting that he was plied with more liquor than appropriate. Willie saw nothing amiss, so continued to swallow all that was offered, entertaining the company with his choicest songs and stories, until the table was in a roar. About mid career in his jollification, a messenger entered. The laird withdrew. In a few minutes he returned with a surprised air, saying to the company, and particularly Willie, "Gentlemen, here is a very strange matter. A person has arrived at my house demanding admittance, who insists on it that he is the king."

"Admittance!" roared out Willie, a good deal discomposed, "On no account admit him, laird. Tie the impostor neck and heel, and throw him into the nearest burn! Pack him off instantly."

"Nay, nay, sir, I think we had better admit him, and leave it to you and him to decide which of you has the best claim." And before Willie could say more, James himself was ushered in, exclaiming,

"Where is the impudent varlet that has been assuming my incognito? Are you the knave?" he added, addressing Willie, who now had the most rueful expression of countenance imaginable.

"And if I am," Willie answered, "ye needna mak sic a stramash, nor look sae dooms angry either. Yer royalty's no a whit the worse o' me haven't on for a wee bit, and, guid kens, ye're welcome to't back again, for it doesna fit me. Sae tak it, sir, and muckle guid may it do ye!"

James could contain his gravity no longer, but burst into a loud laugh. "You knave; what put it into your head to practise this imposition? You fairly deceived Whinnyhill."

"Never a bit o' me did that, sir," said Willie, somewhat relieved. "He deceived himsel." To the great amusement of everyone, he related the conversation he overheard, concluding, "So ye see, sir, he made me a king whether I wad or no, and, as he put on the coat, I just wore't, although it was like to cost me dear in Middlemass."

"I've heard of that too, sirrah," the king, again laughed, "and it is for the good service you did me there, that I now feel disposed not to hang you." He threw a well-filled purse towards Willie. "There, sirrah, take that, and be gone; but mark me, my royal brother, do not try this prank again, else our quarrel may be a more serious one another time."

Glad to get off on such favourable terms, Willie sneaked out of the apartment without any further remarks, next day setting out on his return to his native district, forswearing kingcraft, and the kingdom of Fife, for ever.

Retold by Richard Wilson

Rattling Roaring Willie companion piece

Rattlin' and roarin' – with just a grain of truth

Rattling, Roaring Willie: a balladeer celebrated in ballad, a murdering minstrel mythologised in music, poetry and song.

He was real enough – and remains so in the poetry of our finest, including Robert Burns and Sir Walter Scott, and in contemporary folk music. Take your pick from the Dubliners, the late Ewan McColl, the Wild Irish Lasses and many more.

A late 16th, early 17th century minstrel, William Henderson of Priesthaugh is our man: a well-known and popular Borders minstrel. Renowned for his fiddle playing, he entertained the good people of Hawick, Jedburgh, Kelso and surrounding villages.

For the sake of the Tale it is understandable that Wilson chooses to highlight the more jovial side of Rattlin's character, making only passing reference to the minstrel's willingness to 'bite'; but we have cause to take the opposite approach, for to describe him as 'pugnacious', as Wilson does, is something of an understatement.

On a fine Spring morning two minstrelling pals meet at their favourite drinking hole at Newmill-on-Teviot about five miles southwest of Hawick. By midday they are drunk, by mid-afternoon they are in dispute, by mid-evening they have brawled themselves into a nearby field and one of them is dead in a duel. In a meadow known locally as Allanhaugh, where the Allan Water and Teviot meet, Rattlin' has committed murder most foul: he has run his sword through his fellow balladeer, William Elliot (otherwise known as Sweet Milk or Robert Reull).

Initially, Rattlin' does what any clear thinking murderer would do: he goes into hiding. It doesn't last long. With restless fiddle-playing hands and a minstrel's yearning for an audience, he heads for Jedburgh's annual Rood Fair. That is his second mistake. The first was spilling Sweet Milk's blood. Rattlin's problem wasn't the murder so much as the fact that Sweet Milk was an Elliot. The Elliots were a reiving clan, and vengeance was the inevitable reaction.

The only surprising aspect of the reivers' revenge was that when Rattlin' was apprehended by two of their number, Gilbert and Archibald Elliot, they didn't commit the act themselves. Instead, they handed him over to the authorities. Following due process and trial at Jedburgh in December 1627, Rattlin's roarin' was brought to an end by hanging. He would fiddle no more, except in the music and song of the centuries to come.

For 150 years Rattlin's memory lived on through oral tradition in the Borders ballad aptly titled Rattling Roaring Willie. In this song, the minstrel heads to the fair to sell his fiddle, finds he can't part with it when the moment comes, is apprehended, and after execution is fondly remembered by the Borders lassies who knew him well.

Burns was the first to put it into print in 1788, when it appeared in The Scots Musical Museum. It is Burns' version you'll hear if you listen to the Dubliners' rendition or indeed most (possibly all) of the countless others available on your music streaming service. Listen as hard as you may, you'll learn nothing of Rattlin's crime, capture or fate. The reason is that Burns directs us to another Rattlin' altogether: William Dunbar, a lawyer friend, who was a confidant and source of encouragement to the poet. Dunbar was 'colonel' of an Edinburgh club, the Crochallan Fencibles, of which Burns was a member. It is the lawyer to whom Burns dedicates his version, as is apparent in the final verse (boord-en' meaning table-end):

> *As I cam by Crochallan*
> *I cannily keekit ben*
> *Rattlin, roaring Willie*
> *Was sittin at yon boord-en'*
> *Sitting at yon boord-en'*
> *And amang guid companie;*
> *Rattlin, roarin Willie*
> *Ye're welcome hame to me.*

Sir Walter Scott's version is closer to the oral-tradition ballad, and he also makes reference to the Allanhaugh murder in another of his works, The Lay of the Last Minstrel (1805):

> *But he, the jovial Harper, taught*
> *Me, yet a youth, how it was fought,*
> *In the guise which now I say;*
> *He knew each ordinance and clause*
> *Of Black Lord Archibald's battle laws,*
> *In old Douglas' day.*
> *He brooked not, he, that scoffing tongue*
> *Should tax his minstrelsy wrong*
> *Or call his song untrue:*
> *For this, when they the goblet plied,*
> *And such rude taunt had chaff'd his pride,*
> *The Bard of Reull he slew.*
> *On Teviot's side, in fight they stood,*
> *And tuneful hands were stain'd with blood;*
> *Where still the thorn's white branches wave,*
> *Memorial o'er his rival's grave.*

Note 'jovial Harper' in the first line, from which it is not unreasonable to speculate that Wilson's identical description of Rattlin' has Scott's poem as its source. The 'thorn's white branches' refers to a tree planted on the spot where Sweet Milk was slain – whose branches continued to wave deep into the 18th century. Another Scottish author and poet also tells Rattlin's tale in print. He is Allan Cunningham, whose version (probably based on Scott's) is in his The Songs of Scotland, Ancient and Modern (1825). Here are the final two verses, damning Rattlin's captors and lamenting his demise:

Now may the name of Elliot
Be cursed frae firth to firth!
He has fettered the gude right hand
That keepit the land in mirth.
That keepit the land in mirth,
And charm'd maids' hearts frae drool;
And sair will they want him, Willie,
When birks are bare at Yule.
The lasses of Ouseman water
Are rugging and riving their hair,
And a' for the sake of Willie –
They'll hear his sangs nae mair.
Dance Teviot's maidens free:
My curses on their cunning,
Wha gaured sweet Willie die!

What, then, of Wilson's Tale? Might an initially inadvertent, innocent case of identity theft contain at least a hint of historical truth? In a word, no. The life of James V was short, a mere 30 years from 1512 to 1542, and he was dead a good 85 years before the noose tightened around Rattlin's neck.

From a distance of almost 500 years, James's reign is largely forgotten outside academic circles. He wasn't even halfway through his second year when, in September 1513, he became Scotland's seventh Stewart monarch. For the nation, the circumstances of his succession could hardly have been more traumatic. From an impregnable position on Flodden Hill his father, James IV, had recklessly led the best of Scotland to a weaker spot on Branxton Hill, near Etal, on the south side of the Border. From there, he and they went to their death in battle against the auld enemy. Shortly afterwards baby James V was crowned at Stirling Castle, destined to become Scotland's ill-loved king and to hear Rattlin's sweet fiddle only in Wilson's imagination.

There are, however, a couple of aspects of the Tale which contain a kernel of truth worthy of comment. The first is Rattlin's sardonic observation when the true king's identity is revealed: "I'm sure yer royalty's no a wit the waur o' me haen't it for a wee bit; and guid kens, yer're welcome

Portrait of James V

till't back again, for it disna fit me. Sae tak it, sir, and muckle guid may't do you." They are words that, had James ever heard them, might have given him cause to reflect. To borrow from the Bard, Henry IV's rueful observation "Uneasy lies the head that wears a crown" springs to mind.

James's four immediate predecessors all suffered untimely, violent deaths and the same is true of his successor daughter. Starting with his great-great grandfather: James I was assassinated by his nobles in 1437; James II accidentally blasted himself into the next life as he stood beside one of his much-loved canons at the siege of Roxburgh in 1460; James III died at the battle of Bannockburn in 1488 (later renamed as the battle of Sauchieburn to distinguish it from the 1314 battle of Bannockburn) in a rebellion in which his son and heir was heavily implicated; James IV died at the hands of an English army at Flodden in 1513; and Mary Queen of Scots was executed at Fotheringhay Castle in Northamptonshire in 1587. James died an unpeaceful death in his bed in December 1542 – it was said of a broken heart on learning of his army's defeat, once again to the auld enemy, at the battle of Solway Moss.

The other aspect of the Tale which deserves a few words is the plot device of one character assuming the identity of another, of which Wilson was very fond. The Royal Bridal (retold in the Revival Edition Vol 5), in which James' father adopts the guise of an itinerant 'gaberlunzie' or beggar, is an example.

In our Tale, Rattlin' taking on the identity of his king is an ironic twist on James' known habit of mingling incognito among the common people. He was known as the Gudeman o' Ballengeich. Why he developed this and other guises is a matter for conjecture. The usual explanations are his hatred and suspicion of the nobility, by whom he had been treated appallingly in his minority, and what we might euphemistically call his roving eye. However, kindness towards an unloved, mostly forgotten king demands we take a more sympathetic view and conclude it was his fondness for the poor and downtrodden which drove James to adopt his gaberlunzie guise. There is as least some evidence of his willingness to embrace those whom others might have cast out, such as his genuine affection for the Kirk Yetholm gypsies and their Faa king.

For more, you can do no better than spend a little of your hard-earned cash on the purchase of Revival Edition Vol 6, where you'll find The Faa's Revenge among other fine Tales.

Background by Keith Ryan

The Monk of St Anthony

In the Coal Hill, the most ancient and filthy quarter of Leith, was a hostelry, 'The Ship'. This house was of good repute, much used by the seafarers. Known not only for good cheer and reasonable charges, but also for the landlord, David Wemyss. With all David's civility he also had a spice of good-humoured roguery. His small trickery contained as much to laugh at as to deprecate. In his dealings with guests or customers he was always obliging and conscientious. He knew this to be for his interest, and therefore did he abide by it.

In the year 1559 the Reformation had not yet driven papacy entirely out of the land, though had compelled it to retire into holes and corners, avoiding the public eye. Monks still moved stealthily and crestfallen through the streets of Leith, to and from one of their last retreats, the preceptory of St. Anthony, at the western end of Kirkgate.

On an evening in May, mine host of 'The Ship' was suddenly summoned from tapping a new hogshead of claret by a gentle rap at the quiet back door which stood beside the cellar hatchway. He admitted a Friar, Peter Drinkhooly, who glided into the little dark closet, and was offered a sample of the new butt. The Father, readily accepting the gratifying invitation, seized the tankard, and, at one pull, emptied it of half its contents. He replaced the vessel on the table, wiped his mouth with a quiet, composed air, and, in a soft undertone, said, "Fair liquor, David, fair liquor. What size is the cask?"

"It's a gey thumper, big aneugh, I hope, to see oot the siege o' Leith. Heard ye if there hae been mony killed the day?"

Although he cared little for either the new religion or the old, David was suspected of a leaning towards the latter, but this was a point not easily decided on, for the very accommodating nature of David's doctrines could quickly adapt themselves to any circumstances.

"Alas! a very great number. There has been a terrible slaughter today at the western block-house. The brethren and I have shrived some twenty or thirty departing souls, who fell by the cannon-shot of the enemy. Two of them officers and men of rank in the French army; worthy, pious men who have left something considerable to the brotherhood. But God knows if we will be permitted to enjoy it. Here," continued the worthy father, drawing out a leathern bag well stored with coin, "here are a hundred and fifty crowns placed in my hands by one of these dying Christians, and here are three gold rings, worth fifty merks each, that were given unto me by the other, under pledge of saying fifteen masses for the well-being of the soul of the departed donor."

"My feth! no a bad day's work," said David. "The siege is no like to be such a bad job for ye, after a'. But here's to ye, father, and Gude send us mair peacefu' times."

Mine host cleared off the tankard. Brother Drinkhooly peered into the empty vessel with a half involuntary spirit of inquiry. In half a minute after another tankard reamed on the board. By the time this generous supply was exhausted, brother Drinkhooly was exhibiting odd changes of manner. From being solemn and taciturn, he became energetic and talkative, with boldness and vivacity which contrasted with his demeanour but half an hour before. Finally he was so overcome that he did not think it would be to the credit of the preceptory to return until he had had an hour or two's sleep.

"Indeed, I dare say ye'll no be the waur o't," said mine host.

Always especially tender of customers in the helpless condition of Peter, David conducted, or rather, smuggled, him into a small back bedroom, helped him off with his gown and shovel hat, and tumbled him into bed, where he left him, with a promise to awake him at the expiry of two hours. Shortly afterward David was attracted to the door by an alarming outcry on the street. On looking out, he saw a boy approaching and bawling out,

"A priest, a priest! For the love o' God, a priest to shrive a dying sinner. A priest, a priest! For a French offisher that has just been struck wi' a cannon-shot on the ramparts."

"Doon wi' the man o' sin!" shouted another.

"Pu' Papery frae its throne o'iniquity!" exclaimed a third.

"Strike your spurs into your horse's sides, and let us shew them clean heels for it," said the leader of the party, now beside David and speaking in a low but firm and earnest tone.

He did as he said, and his men likewise, carrying themselves clear of the crowd. Their unhappy charge, being no horseman, was unable to follow. Before he could explain the facts of his case, a well-aimed brickbat took him on the right temple, and tumbled him senseless from his horse. The mob, suddenly appalled by this catastrophe, and imagining that the unhappy man was killed outright, stood aloof for a few seconds. David, almost instantly recovered from the stunning effect of the blow, started to his feet, and finding the press slackened around him pushed his way through it, and took to his heels. This was the signal for a general chase. Released of responsibility for a murder, the mob chased David down Leith Wynd, and he would maybe escape, had he not lost his feet and fell, with dreadful violence, on his face, several pursuers tripping over him. Those who fell now instantly betook themselves to avenging their fall by tearing and worrying at the unlucky cause of their accident, while others coming up added to his punishment by merciless kicks and buffets, that deprived him of all consciousness. At this critical moment a person approached, asking what was the meaning of the uproar.

"They're bastin a Papist--a fat priest o' Baal, they hae gotten hold of," said a burly fellow who appeared to be a shoemaker. "Giein him a taste o' Purgatory, just by way o' seasonin."

"What? is this more of the accursed doings of the persecutors of the church." exclaimed the stranger, deeply indignant. Drawing his sword, he rushed into the crowd, calling out, "Stand aside, ye caitiffs! shame on ye. Would ye murder a defenceless man? Would ye bring Heaven's wrath upon yourselves by so foul a deed?"

The crowd drew back, and seeing David still living he spoke again,

"Ten crowns to any three or four of ye who will bear this man with me to the south of the city."

At length, a brawny-armed smith, with shirt rolled up to his shoulders, stepping out of the crowd, answered.

"Well, I'm your man for one. Bob, and you Archy," he continued, selecting two from the mob, "will ye no join us in giein a lift to the carrion? Ten croons are no to be fand at every dike-side."

The unlucky brother was now placed on a few boards, his face dreadfully swollen and disfigured; and the procession moved off, the shouting and laughing mob at its heels.

When Peter Drinkhooly came to from his nap and found himself stripped of his gown he was greatly alarmed. Unable to discover any trace of gown or hat he began rapping on the door to bring some one to his assistance. His gown and hat he must have. He could not leave the house without them, and without assistance they could not be got. Mrs Wemyss appeared.

"Is my good friend David not in the way? He would help me to mine outer covering and head-gear."

"Indeed, no, your reverence, David's no in the way, and I canna tell whar he is. He's been missing oot o' the hous thae three hours, and gaed aff without telling ony o' us whar he was gaun, or what he was gaun aboot. Indeed, nane o' us kent when he gaed. Sae he maun hae slippit aff unco cannily."

So he called for the girl, to send her to the preceptory. She was to ask a private word of Brother Christie, and to say to him that he had got into tribulation. That, having some private matters to talk over with mine host of 'The Ship', he had called, and being overcome with exhaustion in consequence of his fatiguing duties, he had fallen asleep. While he slept some one had removed his gown and hat, and he could not therefore return unless his good brother, Christie, would loan him these two articles, the which, he had no doubt, he would readily do. The girl returned within the quarter hour.

"He said, sir," replied the girl, who was both too young and too single-minded to think of saving any one's feelings at the expense of truth, "that, if ye had drank less claret, ye wad hae kenned better what had become o' your gown and hat."

"And would he not give thee the garments?"

"No, please you, sir; he said ye micht gang without the breeks for him. He wadna send ye a stitch."

So it was equipped with articles from mine host's wardrobe that Brother Drinkhooly slunk through the streets, gained the gate of the preceptory, knocked, whispered words of explanation to a friendly porter, and finally snuck to his own dormitory without detection.

In Edinburgh, it was nearly twelve hours after the tragical affair in Leith Wynd before David returned to consciousness. Consider, if you can, his surprise and amazement to find himself in a superb bed, hung round with rich crimson velvet curtains, with coverlets of satin fringed with gold. The room, also gorgeously furnished, was so darkened when David awoke from a refreshing sleep that it was some time before he discovered all the splendours surrounding him. As David went on with his survey he perceived two objects convincing him that he was in the house of a Roman Catholic. One who still clung to the ancient religion of the kingdom, holding in detestation and abhorrence the new doctrines. The objects were a large painting over the fire-place, of the Saviour on the Cross, and a small silver crucifix standing on a table close by the bed side. Also, lying on the floor near the crucifix, a crimson velvet cushion with gold tassels which showed its having recently been knelt upon.

"'Odd, but this is a most extraordinar and dooms awkward affair," thought David. "Wha wad hae dreamed o't. Wha wad hae dreamed that sae simple a thing as me putting on Drinkhooly's goun wad hae led to a' this mischief?"

At this moment a man entered, and bowing respectfully, said, "I trust, holy father, I find you better. Here is a posset prepared for you by direction of our leech, worthy Dr. Whang o' the Cowgate Head, which you will be so good as to take."

"My man," said David, "I'm misdoubtin that there's a sad mistak in this business a'thegither. Howsomever, let that flee stick to the wa' for the present. Can ye tell me whar I am, and hoo I cam here?"

"Most assuredly, holy father. You are now in the house and under the protection and guardianship of Lady Wisherton of Wisherton Mains. As to the manner of your coming here, holy father, it was this. Her ladyship's son, Lord Boggyland, coming up Leith Wynd last night, found you in the midst of a crowd of sacrilegious ruffians who were murdering you, and had already deprived you of all consciousness. Seeing this his lordship, who is a staunch adherent of the old religion with all his family, instantly interfered in your behalf, and had you conveyed to his mother's house, where you are at the present moment."

"Umph," muttered David. "Is that the way o't. Then, I fancy, I'm juist oot o' the fryin-pan into the fire."

An elderly lady, of tall and majestic form, in a close fitting black velvet dress, entered the chamber. She was adorned with a gold chain round her neck, suspending a large diamond cross. Approaching, with stately step, but with a look of tender concern, she welcomed him,

"It rejoices me much, holy father," she said, "to learn that your reverence begins to feel some symptoms of amendment."

"Ou, thank ye, mem, thank ye," replied David, with no small trepidation, for the dignified and stately appearance of his visiter had sadly appalled him. "I fin' mysel a hauntle better, thanks to your leddyship's kindness, takin' ye to be Leddy Wisherton hersel', as I hae nae doot ye are."

"You are right, good father," replied Lady Wisherton, rather taken aback by the very peculiar style of his reverence's language, which she did not recollect meeting with in any other person in holy orders before. The circumstance only puzzled her. It did not excite in her the smallest suspicion of the real facts of the case. "You are right in your conjecture, good father," she said, "I am Lady Wisherton." Suddenly bursting into a sudden paroxysm of pious excitation she exclaimed "O father!what is to become of our poor persecuted church? When will a judgment descend on this unholy land, for the monstrous sins by which it is now polluted each day. Dreadful times that a priest of God should be attacked on the public streets, and put in jeopardy of his life by a mob of heretical blasphemers! When will these atrocities cease? Oh, when, when, when?"

"Deed, mam, it's no easy sayin. They're awfu' times. Nae man leevin ever saw or heard o' the like o' them. Doon at Leith enow, they're murderin ane anither by the dizzen every day, and no comin a bit nearer the point after a'. Heaven kens whar it's to end. In the meantime, they hae gien me a confounded lounderin."

"You have been sorely abused by them indeed, father," replied Lady Wisherton. "But a day of retribution is coming. You will be avenged, terribly avenged. Was it not a blessing of Providence, father, that my son, Lord Boggyland, happened to be in Leith Wynd at the time you were attacked?"

"It was just that." replied David, "A Gude's mercy. They gied me a bonny creeshin as it was; but they wad hae dished me clean oot an it hadna been for him. Feth, yon fellows care nae mair for a man's life than they wad do for a puddock's."

"Then you shall remain where you are, until you be perfectly recovered, which we dare not hope for under a fortnight, at the very least. But in the meantime, good father, you shall have every attendance, every comfort which you can desire, or of which your situation will admit. My son and I are but too happy for the opportunity of testifying our reverence and love for a minister of our holy religion. As to your fears for any uneasiness among your friends in Leith on account of your absence, be not concerned. I have sent notice to the preceptory, relating all that has happened, saying that you are in my house and in safety. Have no doubt that some of the brethren will be here in the course of the evening."

He was appalled and horrified at this impending catastrophe, but said nothing. Anxious to be alone to think and consider what could best be done, he began to affect drowsiness. His noble hostess, taking the hint, quietly left the apartment. Hearing the door close, David first opened one eye cautiously, and then the other, then turning gently round, peered over the edge of the bed to see if the coast was clear. Discovering that it was, he made an escape by the simple process of stealing out of the house after dark. He was fortunate enough to succeed in his hazardous attempt by dropping from a window a full storey in height, at the back part of the house.

So it came about that about twelve of the clock David Wemyss' worthy spouse was startled by a low tap-tapping at the back door. She had been in great distress at his disappearance, and was now of the belief that he had fallen over the quay and was drowned. Thinking it might be some one with tidings, she instantly got up, lighted a candle, and, apprehensive and alarmed, opened the door to her beloved David. She instantly set up a scream of delight.

"Whisht, whisht, woman," said David, stealing into the back apartment as fast as he could. "This is no a business to blaw about. The calmer sough we keep the better."

"But, gude sake, David," said his wife, after securing the door, "whar hae ye been a' this time, and whar hae ye gotten that awfu-like face?"

"I hae gotten a hantle mair than that, guidwife, although ye dinna see't," he replied, "I dinna believe there's a hale bane in my entire buik. I hae had a bonny time aneuch to serve a man his hale life time since I left ye, yet it was a' crammed into ae four-and-twenty hours. But gie me a mouthfu o' brandy, and I'll tell ye a' about it."

Who the sufferer was for whom he first turned out, he never learnt, nor for obvious reasons, did he ever inquire. David Wemyss always thought the less that was said about the whole business the better, and acting on this opinion, he carefully abstained from ever making it a matter of conversation. But some hints escaped, to the great annoyance of the landlord, and on dark nights some ragged child might shout in at the door of 'The Ship',

"Davie Wemyss gaed oot a priest, By filthy lucre temptit;

Davie Wemyss cam hame again.

And thocht nae body kent it."

and David would feel obliged to rush out with a stick to inflict punishment on the offenders.

Retold by Andrea Williams

The Monk of St Anthony companion piece

This Tale takes place in one of the many chaotic and violent periods that have punctuated Scottish history.

Scotland had usually allied with France, the Auld Alliance, as a bulwark against English dominance. In retrospect Scotland doesn't seem to have benefitted much from this arrangement - witness the Battle of Flodden and other disastrous encounters.

Henry VIII, after severing ties with Rome for purely personal reasons, put pressure on James V, a Catholic monarch in what was still a Catholic country, in order to avoid a counter-reformation starting from his northern neighbour. In 1538, James sailed to France and subsequently married Mary of Guise, widow of the Duke of Lorraine who provided him with a handsome dowry.

Henry continued to harass Scotland and, with the king in poor health, the Scottish army was routed at the Battle of Solway Moss. James returned to Falkland Palace where his wife had recently been delivered of her third child - a girl - called after herself, Mary. Her previous two male children had died. Within days, James was dead and the baby became, at a week old, Mary, Queen of Scots.

James' demise has always puzzled historians. It was thought he suffered from porphyria but is now considered more likely to have had Lesch-Nyham syndrome.

A recurrent feature of Scotland's past has been episodes of the premature death of a king with subsequent child succession and internecine warfare between the noble families squabbling for power and this was to be no different.

During this time the Scottish Reformation was underway driven by the oratory and conviction of preachers such as John Knox. They sought the establishment of the Presbyterian Church, not an extension of the Anglican state version espoused by Henry. He had wished Mary to be betrothed to his son Edward and instigated "the Rough Wooing", a series of attacks to pressurise the Scots. This was resisted as it was seen as a prelude to the annexation of Scotland by its powerful southern neighbour.

Mary of Guise thought it was in the best interests of the country, the young queen and herself, for Mary to go to France. The child-queen sailed for France on 7th April 1548 with her "Four Marys", since remembered in song, as ladies-in-waiting. There she was brought up and eventually married Francis, the Dauphin. Thus, she became the Queen of Scots, the future Queen of France and, potentially, the Queen of England through her grandmother Margaret Tudor, wife of James IV and sister of Henry VIII. It is not surprising that Elizabeth I viewed her as a rival.

At the time of the Tale, Mary was growing up in France and the Scottish court had divided into a Catholic pro-French party centred on Mary of Guise and a Protestant pro-English camp led by the Earl of Arran. After the death of Mary I, Mary Tudor, her successor Elizabeth I seeing the threat to her reign, allied with the Protestant faction. Mary of Guise was supplied with French and Italian troops and fortified Leith as a gateway for more help from France. In response, the Protestant Lords of Congregation as they were called sought help from Elizabeth who sent sixteen vessels with eight thousand troops and siege artillery. This, the Siege of Leith, is the scenario during which David Wemyss gets caught up in events to his detriment.

Mary of Guise moved to Edinburgh Castle where she died in 1560. This may have been the event prompting the secretive mission to get a priest for the last rites that resulted in the inn-keeper's forced journey on horseback out of Leith.

After the death of Mary of Guise, a compromise was achieved. The French no longer had a foot in the Scottish court and a treaty was signed between the three nations Scotland, France and England. A council would govern on behalf of the absent queen Mary and her French husband. It would have a Protestant majority. This council drove through the Scottish Reformation and the establishment of the Presbyterian Kirk.

The death of the Dauphin Francis, Mary's return to Scotland and all that ensued thereafter is a tale for another day.

Mary of Guise' coat of arms can still be seen in the Magdalen Chapel, the Cowgate Edinburgh and on the wall of the South Leith Parish Church.

Coal Hill, the Kirkgate, and the old main thoroughfare, are part of the Leith conservation area.

St Anthony's Preceptory or Monastery is still recalled in St Anthony's Street, Place and Lane adjacent to the Kirkgate. The monastery was damaged in the siege and after the Reformation allowed to decline and gradually was demolished.

The Seal of the Preceptory of St Anthony, used to authenticate official paperwork of the monastery and dating from the mid-1500s, is held at the National Museum of Scotland.

On Leith Links there are two mounds, the Giant's Brae and Lady Fyfe's Brae that are said to be the emplacements for the siege guns sent by Elizabeth to the Protestant lords.

Of Lady Wisherton no trace can be found though David Wemyss had reason to be grateful to her.

Background by Michael Fenty

Giant's brea

The Lost Heir of the House of Elphinstone

There was a Doom on the House of Elphinstone. The curse had supposedly been laid at the door of the House by an anguished woman who was determined that 'the sword would never be off the race' until the clan head 'had wedded a maiden of low degree' and their pride humbled. Gossip had it that her motive probably lay in the seduction of an innocent in an earlier time, when Elphinstone pride had scorned the victim. More rational thought suggested that depraved characters could occasionally be seen in great houses for two or three generations. However, ill-fortune, whether attributed to the Doom or not, had certainly tried the Elphinstone clan; at the time of civl war 'Some fell in battle; some bled on the scaffold, and when others ceased to kill them, they began to put an end to themselves'.

This latter statement proved to be the case with Edward, the Laird's second brother. This unhappy young man was found in the woods having ended his life by blowing his brains out.

The narrator of our tale, an elderly gentleman called Plainworth had been a life-long friend of William Elphinstone, the Laird's youngest brother and the eponymous lost heir. Plainworth was an expert on the life of William, who had been the Laird, had 'wedded a maiden of low degree', produced children, and eventually died. Plainworth was one of a group of worthies who regularly met to exchange views gossipy and profound, whilst the glass circled round. During one such meeting talk centred on roving and returning. Determined to relate the tale of William, now that he had died, Plainworth endeavoured to cap all the others stories with William's amazing happenings. This is that Tale.

In earlier times the Elphinstone family was three brothers, the Laird, the unfortunate Edward, and William. There was also a cousin who was, quite simply, a bad man. This cousin had a claim on the estate and was determined to become the Head of the House of Elphinstone. With the demise of Edward, only the Laird and William stood in his way, so he plotted and planned and schemed to achieve his ends.

Although in poor health the Laird was determined to secure the succession, so he kept William close by him and arranged an advantageous marriage for his brother with an heiress of a good family. This lady was very eager to marry William but William was in love with Mary Constant, and therein the Doom begins its work.

Mary was totally without fortune. She was a maiden of low degree, though a sweet girl with high moral values. She loved William dearly but was prepared to sacrifice her own happiness by urging him to gratify his elder brother and marry the lady chosen for him. This was the first time the brothers had been at loggerheads and the wicked cousin saw a chance to increase the rift between the two. He set about besmirching Mary's spotless reputation by spreading the rumour that she had encouraged the advances of a notorious libertine, Sir Charles

Ranger. The cousin reasoned that the Laird would not countenance William's wishes. He supposed William would remain staunchly true to Mary, creating such a bitter quarrel between the brothers that there could be no hope of reconciliation. William would then be sure to leave as the brothers could not then live together in harmony. With the Laird's health so precarious and William out of the way, the fiendish cousin would stake his claim to the Elphinstone estate.

William suspected his cousin of creating the rumour and with a good strong branch cut from a tree beat his scandal-mongering relative soundly. Plainworth, as friend and confidant, warned William that a devious devil like the cousin would get his revenge for the indignity he had suffered. William dismissed such warnings, confiding that his wretched cousin could have the inheritance and, with it the curse, if he himself could only be sure of Mary's love and enough to live on.

However, the profligate Sir Charles became involved. William and Plainworth witnessed Mary walking along with Sir Charles, keeping a respectful social distance between them. He gradually drew nearer to the girl while she, annoyed by his attentions, tried to avoid him. When he eventually grasped her by the arms she screamed, galvanising William into noble action. Leaping over the hedge bordering the track , he grabbed Sir Charles and flung him to the ground. While Plainworth took care of Mary, William persuaded the recumbent knight to name the wicked cousin as instigator of the plot to dishonour Mary. Sir Charles was not best pleased at his humiliation and muttered about duels at dawn. His complaints to the Laird about the way he had been treated was to have repercussions.

With positive proof about his cousin's perfidy William told Mary how his cousin was responsible for the wheels of gossip turning about her. The two exchanged many passionate words, William claiming his love and Mary urging him to marry his brother's choice for the sake of fraternal peace. William was having none of this and finally Mary, persuaded by his love for her and her own deep feelings agreed to a union when he had spoken with her father.

The Laird was steaming with rage as the result of Sir Charles's complaints, and added insult to injury by calling Mary 'improper society'. This slur to his lady riled William into a fierce argument, with the laird angrily stating, 'after this insolence we can never meet more'. The rift between the brothers had opened. Was the fiendish cousin's plan beginning to work? Would William have to leave?

Mary's father was more than happy to agree to an engagement though, so, full to the brim with happiness, William wrote immediately to his brother explaining everything that had happened; 'asking for nothing; apologising for nothing, and concealing nothing'. Next day he went into the town to meet Plainworth. News had leaked and William was heartily congratulated. Being a good natured chap he was persuaded to remain at the inn with Plainworth, despatching an invitation to Mary's father to join them in the celebrations although it was clear he would have preferred to be with his sweetheart.

His encounter with Sir Charles Ranger came under discussion with differing views being expressed about his actions. William gave the company a full explanation of the affair and declared that he would defend any young woman who was the object of unwanted attentions. He further stated that he was more than duty bound to defend the honour of the lady to whom he was betrothed. William confided later that the only impediment to his contentment was the quarrel with his brother. Plainworth tried to assure him that he and his brother would soon be reconciled. This assurance may not have worked, because as he explained many years later, a need to be alone and away from the warmth of the place, prompted him to tell Plainworth he would be speedily back, and he left using the back way.

No sooner had he gone than Mary's father arrived by the front entrance with the news that the Laird had been heartened by William's letter and not only had decided to remove his opposition to the marriage but would like it to take place as soon as possible. How William would have rejoiced! But, where was he? Time passed and he was still absent so the two men went out to search for him. They shouted but answer came there none. The evening was peaceful, with only faint noises coming from the sea. By the light of the rising moon they could just see a two masted lugger crowding on sail with another vessel seemingly in pursuit. Of William there was no sign. He seemed to have vanished off the face of the earth leaving only his hat behind, hanging on a peg.

A diligent search was to no avail, leaving his brother the Laird thoroughly miserable for having parted without reconciliation. Mary was dejected almost beyond reason, but remained true to her family name - Constant. Mayhap the wicked cousin finally achieved his ends, for even to the meanest intelligence, it was clear that William had been kidnapped and was a prisoner on the lugger.

Years passed and the weakly Laird finally died, clearing the way for the cousin to stake his claim. Plainworth was an executor of the estate but despite there being another claimant, there was nothing he could do and after a long litigation, the case went in favour of the wicked cousin. It seemed he was to achieve his ambition to become head of the House of Elphinstone.

William was the lost heir. Years slipped away and we find Plainworth again back in the inn sitting over his drink in a state of dejection over the cousin's successful claim when who should appear at his side but the missing William, in the flesh, looking a veritable tattie-bogle in soaking rags; his features wasted, care worn and woefully sad. Everyone was amazed! Some looked afraid as if William were a phantom. William's first concern was for Mary and whether she was still single. His second question was for his brother, hearing of his death brought forth sad tears. His third concern was for the other men who had just been shipwrecked with him.

After all had been sorted William, freshly clothed and now wearing his old hat, went off with Plainworth to meet Mary and her father. Great was the joy when the lovers were reunited.

You will recall that Plainworth was enticed to relate this story to his group of friends sitting around their glasses gossiping on the topic of 'roving and returning'. William had returned, but his roving had been enforced. His prolonged absence had to be explained, so Plainworth was obliged to set forth what had happened to him whilst away.

William had fully intended to return from his walk that long ago night but strange sounds from the sea side aroused his curiosity and led him to investigate. Smuggling was taking place. Now the kidnap of William was clearly on the smugglers' agenda for he heard them say, 'the very man we want.' The cousin had employed them to get William out of the way and remove one more obstacle to his inheritance claim.

William did not know until much later that the captain of the smugglers' vessel was in cahoots with a notorious pirate called Gonsalvo. This barbarian had his base in the West Indies. Further, the smugglers had a letter from the wicked cousin to Gonsalvo requesting that William be taken into semi-imprisonment on the islands and eventually disposed of. So over the years the depths of his cousin's depravity was gradually revealed; smuggling, kidnap and association with a most brutal pirate.

To meet up with Gonsalvo, they sailed North and into the Atlantic. During the long weeks of sailing many of the crew gained a liking and respect for William, for his innate decency was a quality unfamiliar to them. When they eventually arrived in the West Indian seas they were accosted by the pirate and William learned how the smugglers traded provisions for contraband such as sugar and rum. It was here that members of the smuggling crew gave him positive proof about his cousin's long association with the free-booting trade.

William was considerably alarmed when he was moved to Gonsalvo's vessel and duly shipped to a maze of islands where many captured vessels awaited possible destruction. He now had no compunction about removing many Spanish books from Gonsalvo's cabin before being cast ashore, a virtual prisoner, as the islands were fully under the pirate's brutal control.

He estimated that he remained in the West Indies for four years, more or less alone. He had the use of a small boat for fishing, which he used to explore the islands thoroughly, finding a secret place accessible only when the tides were favourable. He also, with the help of the purloined books, taught himself Spanish. With his knowledge of the islands he planned an escape but needed a vessel much larger than his modest fishing boat. Now, when he was kidnapped he had about him a fair sum

of gold which he had managed to keep hidden and now it was to become useful. Knowing where he could find a suitable vessel he made his way to its anchorage and asked the men on board whether he could buy it. As William's incredible luck would have it, these jolly sailormen were more than easy going. They didn't own the vessel but were quite happy to oblige a young chap offering them gold. They even went so far as to help him sail it into his secret harbour and for a further sum of gold they provided him with all that was needful for a voyage. During the weeks this took they all became friendly due, probably, to William's ability to be an all round good fellow.

He had befriended a widow and her son during his time in the islands. The lad had even gone out fishing with him occasionally. It seemed as if Gonsalvo had forgotten his existence, and this made for carelessness on William's part. Finding from the widow that her son had joined the pirates and betrayed him he knew he had to make good his escape with all due speed. He took himself off to a high point where he could observe Gonsalvo's movements as the barbarian searched for him. While daydreaming of escaping he drifted off to sleep, awaking to English voices. Surrounding him was part of the smuggling crew who had kidnapped him. The better part as it happened. They had fled from the capital crime of gun smuggling and been taken up by Gonsalvo. Though their lives may have been wicked the depth of Gonsalvo's depravity sickened them forever and made them wish to reform themselves and try to return home. The turning point was the fate of a young woman who had fallen into the hands of the pirates and, 'died under their outrages', being afterward flung into the sea 'like a soiled garment'.

This abomination was the final straw. One of the smugglers, Tom Clewgarnet and six of his shipmates determined to amend their lives. They had come up to William's high point in order to view the geography of the islands and see if there was any obvious way of escape. Good fortune favoured both parties: William had a fully equipped ship waiting for a crew and the smugglers had found a man they respected with a means of escape. Surely the Hand of Providence.

Tom Clewgarnet was agitated because the pirates had another girl and her father in their power. He knew that this girl would also be abused unless speedy action was taken. From their high point the party watched Gonsalvo, two attendants and the struggling girl in a boat moving to shore. Knowing the islands intimately, William guessed where they would come ashore so he and Tom ran to the place and waited. When the pirates landed William stabbed Gonsalvo and he and Tom made short work of the two attendants. Although reeking with blood, William was able to reassure the terrified girl that she was in honest hands. Yet again, William had shown honourable behaviour in the protection of women. The rest of the smugglers joined them and all was now in train for a removal on the fishing boat to the larger vessel and escape. But the girl, Carolina, refused to leave without her father, Don Pedro, a Spanish gentleman.

Releasing this man from a ship full of over two hundred armed ruffians might seem an impossible task but by boldness and effrontery William accomplished the deed. He clothed himself in Gonsalvo's bloody garments, covered them with a cloak, left Carolina in the care of Tom and set off with the rest of the men in the dead pirates' own boat. When he arrived within hailing distance he boldly demanded that they hand over Don Pedro, claiming to have Gonsalvo's authority. This ruse paid off and Don Pedro was given into William's charge. The pirates were not daft though, and soon suspecting a trick, they opened fire and gave chase. William's intimate knowledge of the islands enabled him to first find shelter from the guns, then rejoin Tom and Carolina and eventually reach the hidden ship.

As they were just finishing readying the ship and getting water on board Don Pedro reported the pirates on the horizon. Instantly setting forth they made an eleventh hour escape. Once on the open seas they sailed for Don Pedro's home in Havannah. With quiet seas William and Don Pedro became friends, exchanging their personal histories. They were given a great welcome in Havannah and Don Pedro's assurance of safety despite England being at war with Spain and France. The Spanish decided to put paid to the pirates barbarous activities once and for all and William and his men participated, freeing the islanders from the despotic tyranny they had suffered for so long, and being rewarded by the Spanish for their actions.

Staying in Havannah long enough to see Carolina married to her long term betrothed, they set off once more , on board a government packet bound for Cadiz. William and his men were now well set up financially with their pay for the part they had taken in dealing with the pirates. From Cadiz they made their way overland to Antwerp. With letters from Don Pedro, they were able to pass safely despite the war. Antwerp being neutral they were then able to purchase a sloop and sail straight for home. Fortunately, when the sloop sprang a leak they found themselves wrecked, as it were, on their home shore.

Much happened that night; William's shipmates were all rescued and told hair raising tales of their adventures, all being loud in praise of William as their deliverer. Anything of value they had rescued from the wreck and many friends joined the little group at Mary's home. The Lost Heir of the House of Elphinstone had returned to claim his inheritance.

But, what of the wicked cousin? It was fortunate that he was not due to take possession of the estate until the very next day! A plot was hatched involving William making his first public appearance at the moment the wicked cousin came into the house. All were happy to keep the secret. William, showing again that nobility which betokens a true hero, took Plainworth aside to ask that his cousin should be allowed to escape. He had no wish to see a member of his clan suffer on the scaffold for his evil deeds.

Plainworth went to Elphinstone house and found suitable gentlemanly clothes so that all would recognise William despite the long passage of time which had changed his physical appearance. The next day, William was dressed and eventually persuaded to leave Mary's arms and conducted to a chamber in Elphinstone house by the back door. He was locked in and the scene was set for a long overdue public humiliation for the cousin. With all the arrogance of possession he duly entered with the sheriff and officers of the law, demanding his rights. He was given the key to the chamber where William was and told that therein lay the only obstacle to his immediate possession. Once the door was opened, William walked out and was greeted with great delight by all. In the brief confrontation which followed between the two relatives, William was able to convey his forgiveness and pity but also a veiled warning: 'there is intelligence from the other side of the Atlantic, which concerns you more nearly than any further interest which you can possibly have in my inheritance'. The wicked cousin was thus made fully aware that William knew of his association with Gonsalvo, but no one else knew the meaning of the words; William had yet to tell his adventures, thus giving his cousin a chance to escape. Which he did, despite later being pursued by the officers of justice and was never heard of more.

Two weeks later, Mary and William were married, with Plainworth as best man. The Doom on the house had finally been worked out for, as far as folk at the time were concerned William had indeed married, 'a maiden of low degree'.

Retold by Christine Fletcher

Lost Heir of Elphstone companion piece

Greed, retribution and love in a dangerous age

This is a fictional yarn set in the era when rampant smuggling was waning as the Crown increased its efforts to combat illegal trade. It is a tale within a tale encompassing greed, retribution and of course love: a swashbuckling romp probably drawing inspiration from a variety of sources. At about this time Thomson's friend and mentor, Sir Walter Scott, had written Guy Mannering; Byron had published The Corsair; and the reputation of John Nisbet at Gunsgreen House in Eyemouth would have been well known in the Borders region. The Hon William Fullerton Elphinstone of Carberry held the offices of Director and Chairman at the East India Company, whose trading empire encompassed the world and was nearing the zenith of its success.

Author: Reverend George Thomson

George was the son of a Melrose minister of the same name. Born in or about 1792, he was the eldest of seven children, with three brothers and three sisters. He was educated at Edinburgh University and licensed by the Presbytery of Selkirk. Like his father he enjoyed a reputation for kindness, honesty, geniality and eccentricity.

In early childhood he lost a leg to injuries sustained in a wrestling game. But he was blessed with a robust constitution and is said to have demonstrated both vigour and resilience by walking 40 miles from Melrose to Edinburgh on his prosthetic leg. He climbed the Eildon Hills and was once spotted leaping over tombstones in the abbey churchyard.

George became a tutor to Sir Walter Scott's two sons at Abbotsford in 1812, initially walking between Abbotsford and his home in Melrose each day. He quickly became part of the family, who called him Dominie Thomson, and moved into the family home to perform chaplaincy duties in addition to his tutoring.

Sir Walter was quite taken with George, in part due to having pains in his own legs from having suffered with polio in infancy. But he was not blind to his chaplain's limitations. During one Abbotsford Hunt in late October, when 30 to 40 people sat down to dine, Scott was noted to be fiddling impatiently with his spoon as the Dominie performed his role in his usual rather longwinded manner. We see this tendency in the telling of his original Tale!

By 1820 Sir Walter's two sons were grown and Thomson had moved on from Abbotsford. Despite Sir Walter's efforts on his behalf, Thomson was unable to secure a ministry of his own and ended up accepting a tutoring role with another family.

His father died in 1835, the same year Thomson took up his final teaching post in Edinburgh. Three years later he himself was found dead one morning, aged 47, his eccentricity confirmed by the discovery of 100 gold sovereigns hidden in the socket of his wooden leg.

The Elphinstone family

The Elphinstone clan can trace their genealogy back to the beginning of the 13th century. Two volumes of The Elphinstone Family Book of the Lords of Elphinstone, Balmerino and Coupar detail their evolution from 1200 to the death in 1915 of the Honourable Edward Charles Buller Elphinstone. The name continued through a different lineage with Alexander Mountstuart Elphinstone, who is the current 19th Lord Elphinstone and fifth Baron Elphinstone.

The Hon William Elphinstone married Miss Elizabeth Fullerton, heiress of Carberry, in 1774. The Carberry and Elphinstone estates bounded each other and in 1813, following a rise in the family fortunes, the Hon William Fullerton Elphinstone bought Elphinstone Tower which, until then, had been out of family ownership since the 1400s.

While the name William features extensively in the Elphinstone lineage, there are no Edwards until the birth of Edward Dalrymple-Elphinstone in 1877.

Elphinstone Tower

The two primary references to the Elphinstone estates each cite a different Elphinstone Tower. One is a ruin east of Stirling, also known as Dunmore Tower or Airth Tower. It was built in the 16th century by Sir John Elphinstone as the seat of the barony of Elphinstone; Alexander Elphinstone, fourth Lord Elphinstone added a gallery and a new hall before his death in 1638. This estate passed to the Earls of Dunmore in 1754.

The other Elphinstone Tower, four miles southeast of Tranent in East Lothian, is now a dilapidated keep. It was begun in the 13th century but not completed until the 15th: a simple three-storey tower with flagstone flooring and corbelled-out parapet adorned by fearsome gargoyles. There was a cap-house at one corner with open rounds at the others. A mansion constructed beside the keep in the 1600s stood until 1865, when it was destroyed by subsidence caused by local coal workings.

In George Thomson's time this mansion is likely to have been in full use. Given his society connections across the Borders, he may well have visited it on at least one occasion.

Elphinstone Carberry Tower

As with many such constructions, the tower's basement was vaulted. The first floor was also vaulted and housed both the main hall and original kitchen, which was screened by a partition. The private chambers were housed on the upper levels. Within the thick stone walls a number of small discrete rooms and stairs were constructed, including a spyhole behind a fireplace from where the hall could be watched in secret and safety.

A legend persists that there was an underground passage linking the tower to Fa'side Castle, about a mile to the northwest.

Smuggling in the early 19th century

Smuggling remained a vibrant activity during the latter half of the 18th century and early 19th century. The golden age of illicit whisky in Scotland stretched from 1725, when the first British malt tax was levied in Scotland, to 1823 when the government found a working tax system that (almost) ended the illegal whisky trade. Between 1707 and 1814 the government inadvertently created an environment which encouraged illegal whisky production and smuggling: the more laws and taxes it introduced, the more it stimulated unlawful activity.

The primary players in this area's smuggling business were a cohort of merchants at home and abroad. Among some 30 merchants identified as working in or from Eyemouth in the period 1740-1790, it is difficult to identify any who were not involved in smuggling, judging by official records such as those held at Collector's Quarterly Accounts for the Customs Centre at Dunbar. Several of the overseas merchants who supplied the smugglers have been identified, and at least some of these were regarded as respectable citizens in their home ports. The most significant player in George Thomson's time will have been John Nisbet, the notorious merchant and smuggler who with his associates conducted operations from Gunsgreen House in Eyemouth. Nisbet had established networks across Europe, most notably in Gothenberg and Rotterdam and from there to almost anywhere else in the known world.

East Lothian's illicit trade from French and Dutch ships was widespread: smuggled goods were frequently discovered in the houses of the middle classes and, perhaps more surprisingly, in those of senior officials responsible for enforcing the law and administering justice.

Smuggling activity along the coastal stretch from Prestonpans to Berwick-upon-Tweed was at its peak in the early 1800s. Taxes aimed at recouping the expenses of the Napoleonic War provided ample motivation to find inventive new ways to 'cheat the King' of his excise duty. Popular goods smuggled at this time included tea, brandy, gin, aniseed, French salt, chocolate, currants and figs, sugar candy, coffee berries, Dutch cotton, Indian handkerchiefs, gunpowder and snuff.

The task of trying to control smuggling and secure revenue collection fell to the Riding Officers working for the Scottish Board of Customs and HM Customs for England and Wales. Located at regular intervals along the coast, they were tasked with patrolling the stretches between the ports on horseback. Each officer was expected to patrol 10 miles of coastline, supported by additional officers in known hotspots. They often found themselves greatly outnumbered by the smugglers, if they were not in fact collaborating with them.

Documents dated September 1729 in the Newcastle Custom House show three vessels patrolling the northeast coast: Cruiser from Flamborough Head to Newcastle, Deal Castle from Newcastle to Leith and Spy from the Firth of Forth to Newcastle. At about this time the Deal Castle is recorded as capturing four French smuggling craft and bringing them into Shields.

By 1797 Customs had a fleet of 33 seagoing cutters covering the coastal waters of Britain. In addition, these vessels were able to request assistance from the Royal Navy to apprehend suspect or evasive vessels. The Navy also assigned several of its own ships to smuggling deterrence and prevention.

In the ports themselves, Customs and Excise officers were organised into the 'water guard' – made up of tide surveyors, tide waiters, watermen and watchmen, and coast waiters. The tide surveyors were under instruction to board 'every ship from foreign parts', assisted by the tide waiters, and make a thorough inspection of vessel and cargo.

Regular visits would continue to be made until all cargo was unloaded, the vessel cleared and the tide waiters withdrawn. The tide surveyors were directed to 'rummage' at every opportunity, a term used since the 17th century to describe the practice of systematically searching a vessel for illicit goods.

During the early 19th century, the organisation of the boats and cruisers (previously run from the local Custom House) was brought together under a new body named the Preventive Water Guard, which was eventually merged with the Riding Officers to create what we now know as the Coastguard.

New York hangings

A review of the recorded hangings available through the New York State archives provides much evidence that the practice was widely used at the time of this Tale. It does not, however, list anyone hung for reasons of piracy – only for murder, robbery, rape and forgery, although arguably any of these might be part and parcel of a pirate life. The name James Stray is not among those recorded.

Don Pedro of Havannah

A merchant by the name of Don Pedro de la Cuesta y Manzanal traded between Salamanca, Havannah and Cadiz in the late 1700s and was connected with the famous German naturalist, explorer and geographer Alexander von Humbolt. A prolific and renowned author, Humbolt was elected a member of the Linnean Society of London in 1818.

The name Pedro was arguably a safe bet in light of the Spanish dominance of Cuba at the time. Equally the choice of name may have been influenced either by the exploits of Pirate Gilbert (1800-1835) as reported in the Scottish press, or by Dom Pedro, Emperor of Brazil (1822-1831) and King of Portugal (1826).

Background by Andrew Leaver; who acknowledges information from the Melrose and Bowden Parish Church newsletter, courtesy of Rev Rosie Frew, and articles by Mrs Margaret Jackson Young published in The Eildon.

The Battle Of Dryffe Sands

Forgetting, or perhaps not caring, about the risks posed by sallies onto others lands, Reiver women were never shy to raise their request for larder supplies by serving a set of clean spurs for supper. One mistress, Lady Maxwell (nee Douglas), of Thrieve Castle was further driven by the need to see the aggrandisement of her husband's family.

In the late 1500s, the ancient hereditary feud between the Maxwells of Nithsdale and the Johnstones of Annandale erupted back into life.

Several of the lairds, whose lands lay within the disputed districts sustained serious injury from the invading Johnstones. To defeat the challengers and preserve their property, they entered into a secret compact, both offensive and defensive, with Lord Maxwell.

Intelligence of the pact reached Sir James Johnstone, who immediately tried to break the league. Protracted petty warfare produced no decisive result, although it seemed the Maxwells were acquiring ascendency over the land. Then Johnstone secured aid from the Scotts, and other clans from the midland district. Lord Maxwell rallied around him the Barons of Nithsdale and thus, by December 1593, the stage was set for the Battle of Dryffe Sands.

A steadfast woman, Lady Maxwell entertained no extravagant dread for the safety of her husband and their son, who departed with her blessing. Indeed, she could barely suppress her impatience for their glorious return.

However, by the afternoon of the second day, still with no intelligence, even she had to check a melancholic train of thought. As the shades of that evening descended she ascended the battlements of their ancient home with her small daughters and younger son.

Thrieve, situated on a small island in the river Dee, is a forbidding island fortress. The situation allows a clear view of the lands around it. Gazing into the twilight she willed her men's return. A band of mosstroopers[1] emerged from the east. The light was still strong enough for her to observe their demeanour. No victorious swagger could be detected. Steeds and men, both exhausted, returned under a silencing blanket of defeat.

Praying that no evil had befallen her party, she had scarcely entered the hall of the castle when alone before her stood her eldest son.

Realising her loss instantly she cried out "Your father! where is my husband?" answering herself in the same breath with "He will return no more…"

The new Lords silence confirmed her fears. Ever a Reiver woman she concealed how sick in her heart and weak in her limbs she felt, retiring to the privacy of her chamber before giving full force to her grief.

In the Baronial Hall, their new master controlled his grief. Occupying the seat of his father he extended the household hospitality in feeding the exhausted company.

The conversation of the diners revealed that the demise of Maxwell Snr, at the Dryffe Sands, in Annandale, was due, not to the prowess of the Johnstones, but the cowardice of those confederates whose alliance had been the sole cause of the renewed hostility.

---

1 *Moss-troopers: were brigands of the mid-17th century, who operated across the border country between Scotland and the northern English counties of Northumberland and Cumberland.*

Struck from his horse, his hand, outstretched in entreaty, was severed before his final merciless slaughter. Many of his followers perished in the fight, more were disabled by the cutting 'Lockerby Licks'[2] of their enemies swords. The new Lord and his friends had now withdrawn to regroup before further prosecuting their enemies in battle.

Lady Maxwell summoned her son to find out their plans.

"Orchardstone[3] talks of a bond." he tells her.

"A bond of alliance! And did you listen to him?" her gaze fixes upon him. "Peace! who would talk of peace to one who has just suffered bereavement? Talk of revenge. Remember, the blood of him so treacherously slain flows in your veins. You had no craven heart from him--none from me. Why so mute and wavering?"

"Madam, you have forestalled me," he replies. "I will have revenge…"

But she interrupts. Mocking him, speaking of the shame she feels, the shame he brings, finally declaring him a coward.

"Madam," he implores, "I am no coward, no craven, nor am I a child that needs to be chidden with the rod or with harsh speeches; my father's blood boils as fiercely in my veins as the blood of Douglas in yours. The deliberations are not over."

"But, my son, you say not that you will seek revenge," she cries; "you speak of those petty barons, whom you demean yourself to consult. Your father told them his will. It was theirs to obey."

"Why do you speak so hardly of me?" he asks. "Have I not borne myself like my equals and my race? You shall not want revenge. This house, these lands, these vassals, are yours, until revenge is yours. No lady shall hold your place; my life shall have but one object till that is accomplished; my being shall have but one end."

---

2 Lockerby Lick: This kind of wound is called a "Lockerby lick"--the place which bears that name being in the immediate vicinity of the field of battle.

3 Orchardstone: Sir Robert Maxwell of Orchardstone was the brother in law to Sir James Johnstone, but was a fully pledged an ally of Lord Maxwell.

"Stay, my son" she asks, her tone calmer. "You have said enough to satisfy my doubts."

Having retired to his chamber and overcome by fatigue he slept until disturbed by an elder clansman, a Presbyterian Minister and relative of his father, a man whose counsel he trusted. He addresses young Maxwell,

"I fear your rest has been broken by my impatience; my anxiety to see you before your comrades were astir left me no choice."

His young friend assured him that refreshed from his sleep he is eager to know the cause of his mentors concern.

The Minister reminds him that Border morality would require his Fathers death be avenged. But he entreats him to use his own judgment, foregoing vengeful desires and resisting the compulsion to be dictated to by others. Instead, he counsels alliance with Johnstone.

"It may not be," the young Lord replies. "My fathers have died on the battle-field. I must not die in my bed. I am bound by a solemn vow to seek revenge, by day and night, by all honourable means; to risk life, lands, liberty and happiness, in this world and the next, before abandoning the pursuit."

"But, my son, you who are dearer to me than life. A vow or oath which has an evil object in view may be honourably discharged only if it is broken." replies the Minister."

"The oath is no longer in mine own keeping; and I would not break it, even if I could."

"Alas!" exclaims the Minister. "I hoped that you might heal the wounds of this distracted land, proving an honour to your people."

"Forgive me, life has been lost, it must be avenged. Perishing on the field of battle, my fathers' blood cries aloud for vengeance."

Grief struck, the old man is left alone as Maxwell joins the barons so all can break their fast. Debate was fierce, division equal as the barons considered whether or not to enter into league with Sir James Johnstone. The young Lord avowed his intention of seeing them act in accord of their letters of manrent[4] and ended the deliberations. Preparations for war began. Sir Robert Maxwell of Orchardstone was permitted to remain inactive, though his men were required to serve.

An intense period of shameful internecine conflict followed. Atrocities were committed; villages were razed to the ground, their occupants discarded like rubbish; mercy and kindness became words of myth with no place in either the land nor its vocabulary.

The heat of the battles tempered the resolve of the young Lord in his pursuit of revenge. His ears were deaf to all pleadings to stop. Not even the King could make his voice heard above the din of the lords internal and vindictive hatred. The appointment of Maxwells' enemy as Warden of the middle Marches, six years after Dryffe Sands, further provoked him greatly.

As a consequence King James provided James Johnstone with a force sufficient to expel the refractory Maxwell. Maxwell, now an outlaw, was more demented in anger than ever.

The Marquis of Hamilton, kinsman to Maxwell, invited him to the family seat of Craignethan Castle. Maxwell made a dour and despondent house guest, only finding respite from his rage when rambling in the country or losing himself in the woods. During one such wander, whilst supine on the forest floor, he heard a song familiar to Borderers. An association was awakened in his mind on hearing 'Johnnie Armstrong's Last Good-night[5]'. It touched his revenge nerve, but he remained ever more enchanted by the sweet voice of the singer. Keen to make her acquaintance he stood up, but found himself alone.

That evening at the Castle, sitting in silence amidst the company, he was asked to adjudge between a French Count and one of his countrymen as to who could best present their country's music. Shaking his head in response he decided instead to try to ascertain the identity of the singer whose tones had lulled him during his afternoon idyll. Enquiring as to who the singer may have been, he suggests

---

4 *Manrent: refers to a Scottish contract of the mid-15th to the early 17th century. Usually military. The bond of manrent was commonly an instrument in which a weaker man or clan or family, pledged to serve, in return for protection, a stronger lord or clan.*

5 *'Johnnie Armstrongs' Last Goodnight':.. Said to have told of one of the Armstrongs, executed for the murder of Sir John Carmichael of Edrom, Warden of the Middle Marches, who bids goodbye to those he loves.*

"A local lass perhaps?"

"No village girl, my lord", exclaims the defender of Scottish music. All eyes fix upon young Lady Margaret Hamilton, whose blushes betray her.

Persuaded by the company she sings once more, 'Armstrong's Last Good-Night'.

Maxwell chides himself. Lady Margaret, endowed with a sweet voice is also possessed of great personal attractions. He had frequently heard her sing, but only when the familiar ballad fell upon his ear was his attention awakened to its singer. Now in her eighteenth year, a raven haired beauty, she has a life force that radiates through her.

And so it was, that one became two on those excursions into the country. Margaret, the informed and informing guide. Her narrative and descriptions giving life to whatever they saw. As they journeyed together and talked so their mutual feelings grew. Until, it could be said, they were in the grip of love.

Maxwell forgot his anger, feuds, animosities and want for revenge. His new engagement melted his old fury, allowing him to express gentle attention and more intellectual pursuits.

Sadly, he could not sustain this peace nor this bliss.

In the autumn, Maxwell, when approached by the Marquis regarding the possibility of his marrying Margaret had his conscience pricked. His honeymoon of sloth and self indulgence at Craignethan Castle ended in an instant. He stood silently until his disconcerted friend seized him by the hand, rousing him from his fearful reverie.

"Thank you," he cries, "but I forgot. Your roof can shelter me no more. I must leave you now--ay, this very instant. You have reminded me of my duty; every moment I stay here is a moment lost."

Pressed by the Marquis about this sudden change in intentions, he answers, "My father's death is unavenged. I have loitered here like a dull slave shrinking from his task. Forfeiting my faith. Breaking my oath. I must redeem the one, and fulfil the other. I shall remain unwedded until my first duty is discharged. Should the fair lady of whom you spoke deign to look down on one so unworthy, she will see me a suitor at her feet."

The Marquis could not change Maxwells resolve. No more than the King could stop wars of hereditary hate. On his return to Thrieve, Maxwell ensured immediate preparations were made to execute an excursion into Annandale.

Sir James had well placed watchers within his territory. Men whose duty it was to enforce the will of the Sovereign and see to it that Maxwell would once more be forced to retire from the Borders. And so, on their alert, selecting rising ground not far from the fateful scene of Dryffe Sands he readied for the attack.

Maxwell, surprised at not taking his opponents unaware and with characteristic impetuosity and hubris, launched into battle (the shame of retreat without engagement worse for him than the risk of mass slaughter).

His followers fought with desperate courage during the protracted engagement but still they were unable to keep their ground against the large and well appointed enemy. Briefly, he rallied them but his efforts were in vain as retainers fled on every side. No defeatist, he rushed into the heart of his adversaries.

On Sir James' order he was taken alive and conveyed to Edinburgh. Immured in the castle, the insult of his capture added to his loss and caused him to ferment his fury.

Margaret Hamilton was residing in Edinburgh during this time. News of his imprisonment grieved her, but his proximity gave some hope and she resolved to try and secure his release. She happened upon his foster brother, Charlie o' Kirkhouse, a man devotedly attached to the young Lord who shared Margarets cause. More a doer than a thinker, Charlie had decided to consult Margaret. She persuaded him to enlist in Royal Service to best place him to take advantage of any opportunity to assist in an escape, or support her in any scheme she might devise. He eventually secured an appointment, despite the objections of Johnstone's wily and suspicious lieutenant Will o'Gunmerlie.

He was on guard in Maxwell's prison one day, when another guard approached, accompanied by a youth whose bonnet mostly concealed his face. Charlie was able to confirm that the youth was Maxwell's brother, thus gaining him admission to Maxwell. "Your brother, my lord," announced the Gaoler. "I will return in half-an-hour."

"My brother Charlie?" said Maxwell, meeting his visitor. "I thought you had been in London. But how…? you are not my brother." Instead of answering, the youth blushed 'celestial rosy red, love's proper hue'

"You have not forgotten 'Johnny Armstrong's Good-night,'" whispered the youth.

"Nor that voice, What good spirit has brought you here, my dear Lady Margaret?"

"Your escape." she replied." Let us change outfits and Charlie o'Kirkhouse will meet and guide you out of the Castle."

He refuses and despite her entreaties and pleas he will not acquiesce.

She repeated her hearts desire, that he forsake his crusade for revenge and devote his energy to his country and those he loves, finally reminding him he will be liberated if he pledges to step back from his plans. Tempted, he hushes her to stop her petitions, arguing that if he follows such a course he will be disinherited. Finally, he promises to her that once he has discharged his obligation, there might be time for their happiness.

Following her visit Maxwell became occupied with projects of escape and began wearing at the mortar to make a means of escape.

One evening, having hidden his efforts from his gaoler, he is surprised when the man does not bring his supper but asks instead, "Would you like to escape, my lord?"

"Charlie o' Kirkhouse." exclaims Maxwell. "How…?"

"Quiet replies his tenant. Let us change dress; I shall remain in your stead."

Although initially reluctant, Maxwell allows himself to be persuaded, accepting that no major harm will befall Charlie if the deed is uncovered. By the following morning he is back at Thrieve. Charlie fared less well, receiving three dozen lashes from Gunmerlie for his part in the deed, before being rudely thrust out of the Castle to find such refuge and help as he could.

Maxwell tried once more to raise the barons of Nithsdale, but times and loyalties had changed; his requests were peremptorily refused. His ire reignited. Eventually the idea of seeking a meeting with his old adversary seems the best plan. Sir Robert Maxwell of Orchardstone agrees to be the broker.

Sir James is accompanied by Will o' Gunmerlie, and Maxwell by Charlie o' Kirkhouse. Gunmerlie sneeringly asks after o'Kirkhouses health, and provokes Charlie to shoot the retainer dead. Johnstone, turning to see what had happened was straightway shot in the back by Maxwell. He lived long enough to absolve Orchardstone of unwittingly being the cause of his death.

Maxwell returned to Thrieve where a large company had assembled hoping to celebrate the planned reconciliation and his marriage to Lady Margaret. To his credit, Maxwell explained to the Marquis what happened and asked him to learn whether, in the circumstance, Margaret will still marry him.

Believing he acted in honour, Margaret is both willing to marry and confident of his securing a pardon from the King.

Despite his bitterness at the truth of his actions Maxwell does not disabuse his fiancee of her view of him. They were wed. The next day, disguised, he fled overseas with Charlie. She wept sweet tears on his leaving, unaware that this would be their Last Goodbye.

Petitions to the King for his pardon failed. Abroad, Maxwell's peace of mind left him. The luxury of time allowed brooding reflection. He never became remorseful but was sanguine on realising his revenge was meanly secured when he shot his enemy in the back.

Four years passed.

His beloved Mary steadfastly waited, wrote and petitioned before starting to fade. Her health finally failed and she died before his return to her side could be realised. Now a widower, he is a fugitive in the wilds of Caithness when he is eventually caught and taken back to Edinburgh castle.

His visitors included the Marquis of Hamilton. But Maxwell, now totally alienated, remained remorseless. Urging him to abandon his self pity, Hamilton offered to mitigate for him before the Court. Maxwell stubbornly refused. Owning only his misery, he was brought before the Court and indicted for murder and fire-raising. Should the later charge be proven the forfeiture of his lands would follow.

He was easily convicted of both crimes and sentenced to be beheaded. All further efforts to obtain a pardon failed.

On the night before his execution Orchardstone visited him with Hamilton.

"And it has come to this at last!" exclaims the old man. "Would you had listened to the prayer of your humble clansman, eighteen years ago. But brief time is left to make your peace. Some holy man may be able to soothe your mind."

"Mock me not, dear uncle," replies Maxwell bitterly. Talk not about peace and holy men. They cannot give me peace or happiness on earth or in heaven." and he continues, "I am content with the share I have enjoyed. One gleam of sunshine has crossed my path. One fair flowret has blessed my sight. One human heart has been mine. My cup of bliss is full--one drop filled it. My heaven has been already enjoyed. Leave me, good uncle, good cousin. I would bless you, but my blessing might prove a curse."

He was beheaded on the following morning, his estates immediately forfeited to the Crown. And so it was, that the Clans of Maxwell and Johnstone, over a period of 20 years, lost their three chiefs to battle, murder and beheading.

Retold by Denise Bradshaw

The Battle of Dryffe Sands companion piece

The Battle of Dryffe Sands was a bloody conflict between Scottish clans of Maxwell, and Johnstone that took place on 6 December 1593, near Lockerbie in Scotland. It was the last large-scale battle fought on the Borders by Borderers. It was a vicious battle, with fighting in the streets of Lockerbie and even today is remembered for the 'Lockerbie Lick', a downward sword cut delivered from horseback to the head of an enemy on foot. The battle was a decisive victory for the Johnstones with a far smaller force of riders but it wasn't the end of the conflict between the families.

The story of The Battle of Dryffe Sands published by Wilson in 1836 is one of the few Border Tales that was anonymous, and it is not so much about the battle itself, but the impact the battle had on the son of one of the key protagonists. It is a story of revenge and lost love, loosely following known facts, and relying heavily on the works of Sir Walter Scott.

In the last quarter of the 16th century organised lawlessness in the Borders had increased to such an extent that by the last quarter of the 1500's there in effect existed a reign of terror. Raids between England and Scotland were bitter and long-drawn out. On either side of the border, Wardens of the Marches were appointed by the Crown, three on each side of the border, east, west and middle. The Wardens were responsible for the security of the border between Scotland and England and for administering the special type of border law known as March law. Until the role was abolished in 1603, the appointments were prestigious, but it often happened that Wardens used their power less for law-keeping, and more for inflicting vengeance on their enemies.

The Maxwells were the most powerful family in south-west Scotland. John the eighth Lord Maxwell served on the Privy Council of Scotland, and was Warden of the West Marches between 1571 and 1577.

The Maxwells were a Roman Catholic family at a time when celebrating the Catholic mass was banned. In 1585 Maxwell had masses sung and said at Lincluden Abbey at Christmas, and for this was imprisoned in Edinburgh Castle and then placed under house arrest in Edinburgh. In 1587, he was given leave to go overseas, travelling to

Madrid where he took part in the planning of the Spanish Armada of 1588. Maxwell returned to Scotland at Dundee and passed into the country in disguise with "a plaid about him, like a wayfaring man." James VI ordered him to surrender his castles of Lochmaben, Langholm, Threave and Caerlaverock. Lochmaben was besieged, and Maxwell was arrested as a traitor. He was placed in the custody of William Stewart of Monkton, then imprisoned in Edinburgh Tolbooth, and later in Blackness Castle, a state prison on the south shore of the Firth of Forth. He was freed in 1589 on a bond of £100,000. In 1592 he was reappointed as Warden of the West Marches.

For many years a fierce feud had been carried on between the Maxwells and the next most powerful family in the district, the Clan Johnston of Annandale which was headed at the time by Sir James Johnston. The Wardenship of the West Marches, recently awarded to Lord Maxwell, had been taken from Sir James Johnstone. Johnstone had been imprisoned in Edinburgh Castle, but escaped and returned home where he and Lord Maxwell were induced to conclude a mutual alliance, binding themselves to support each other in all lawful quarrels.

The Johnstones, on the faith of this treaty, and thinking they had nothing to worry about from the Lord Warden as long as they left the Maxwells alone, raided Nithsdale, committing various attacks on Lord Sanquhar, the Lairds of Drumlanrig, Closeburu, and Lagg, killing eighteen persons. This enterprise so greatly irritated the Government that on the basis of the hereditary feud known to exist between the two families, a commission was given to Lord Maxwell to pursue the Johnstones with the utmost severity of the law.

In December 1593 Maxwell set out from Lockerbie at the head of two thousand men to take the Johnstone stronghold of Lochwood. However, the crafty Johnstone with a far smaller force of riders ambushed Maxwell's advance guard. Maxwell's guard turned and fled headlong into the main body of Maxwell's force who were in the process of crossing Dryffe Sands near Lockerbie. There was great confusion with some of the Maxwell force advancing and some fleeing.

Johnstone and his men were in hot pursuit and continued the battle. The fighting surged into the streets of Lockerbie and Maxwell's disordered men were trapped by the desperate Johnstone riders who cut them down without mercy.

Maxwell himself is said to have been struck from his horse by Johnstone himself, and killed as he lay helpless on the ground raising a hand in supplication. The spot is marked today by two Thorn trees known as the Maxwell Thorns.

Thomas Scrope, the English West March warden, wrote to Lord Burghley on the 7th December 1593, explaining what had occurred the previous day:

> *"Such newes as are credibly advertised unto me furth of Scotland, towching the combers and truble areasen betwixt the Lorde Maxwell and the Larde Johnston, I have thought good to signify unto yow. Yesterday in the afteruone, the Lorde Maxwell with a great force of his frendes, did assemble them selves together, and assaye the dimolishing and casting downe of one Mongo Johnston his howse at Lockerbye : where the Larde Johnston having called together his frendes, did incounter with the said Lorde Maxwell, and haith not only kilde the sayd Lorde Maxwell himself, but verie many of his company. And that as I heare without any great harme to the larde Johnston or his frendes."* Carlisle.
>
> *Signed : T. Scroope. Addressed. Indorsed: "7 Dec. 1593. L. Scroope to my L., advertisinge Maxwels death, slaine by the Larde of Johnston.*

Lord Maxwell was succeeded by his son John, who became the ninth Lord Maxwell. In the Border Tale, John is 'a youth of twenty years' who had fought with his father, whereas in truth, John was only about 10 years old when he inherited the title. About the same time, he was betrothed to Margaret Hamilton, the daughter of John Hamilton the 1st Marquess of Hamilton, and Margaret Lyon, Countess of Cassils, so the description in the Tale of how the two met is a romantic fabrication.

James Maxwell married Margaret by contract dated 9th August 1597 with the marriage being solemnised later. (September). Apparently there were great preparations and purchase of 'rich raiments' in Edinburgh.

Hamilton Palace was palatially decked and the King himself was invited to attend. Sadly the marriage was not a happy one. Eventually the King felt obliged to intervene and James VI wrote to Lord Hamilton on 23 July 1601 that he had persuaded Lord Maxwell 'ane caskart young man' to visit his wife and son (who must have died young).

Reconciliation between Lord Maxwell and the Johnstons was sought by the friendly offices of the Privy Council who prevailed upon Lord Maxwell on 11th June 1605 to issue 'letters of slannis' in favour of Sir James Johnston of Dunskellie. By this document, Lord Maxwell forgave Johnston for the slaughter of his father and all other 'slaughter & mutilations & insolences which followed thereupon.'

However, problems continued. In June 1606 Maxwell was 'put to the horn' ie declared an outlaw, for not setting his wife at liberty and producing her before the Council. Eventually she died during a divorce suit pursued by Maxwell against her. This made the Hamiltons his mortal enemies. The Historian Robert Johnston[1] writing in the late 16th Century, claimed that Maxwells 'harsh treatment had occasioned her death.' However, being of the clan Johnston himself, Johnston may not have been entirely unbiased in his opinion!

On 11th August 1607, Maxwell was again imprisoned in Edinburgh Castle for violence and contempt of the authority of the state. In December that year he teamed up with Sir Seumas MacDonald of Dunvaig, and Robert Maxwell of Dinwoodie. They managed to get their guards drunk in MacDonalds apartments, disarmed them and then locked them in. They then attacked the gate porter and his wife before climbing down the wall to waiting horses. Maxwell got away but MacDonald fell and was recaptured apparently in an attempt to conceal himself in a dunghill.

In the original Border tale, Maxwell's love, Margaret, had visited him in disguise to help him escape. This had a parallel in reality with the escape of William Maxwell, the 5th Earl of Nithsdale, who was a Jacobite supporter sentenced to death for treason on 24 February 1716.

---

1 *JOHNSTON, ROBERT, a Scottish historian, wrote "Historia Rerum Britannicarum, ut et multarum Gallicarum, Belgicarum, et Germanicarum, tam politicarum, quam ecclesiasticarum, ab anno 1572, ad 1628." printed in 1642.*

He made a celebrated escape from the Tower of London by changing clothes with his wife's maid the day before he was due to be executed.

After his own escape, John Maxwell fled to France but later returned to Scotland allegedly with other outlaws and evaded all efforts to capture him. James VI seems to have been infuriated by Maxwell travelling openly accompanied by not fewer than 20 horses to Dumfries and wrote a letter to the Privy Council in December 1607 to issue a proclamation to seize Maxwell's property. The Privy Council indignantly replied that they had used all due diligence to locate Maxwell, and referred to a certain cave to which he used to resort. This is thought to be what is now known as Maxwells Cave on Clawbelly Hill, Blood Moss, Kirkcudbrightshire but there is no visible cave today.

Tired of this uncomfortable life, Lord Maxwell desired to be restored to the King's favour, so in April 1608, sent a message by his cousin, Sir Robert Maxwell of Orchardston, to Sir James Johnston of Johnston (the brother-in-law of the latter), who had expressed a wish for a reconciliation, that a friendly meeting might take place between them. Accordingly, they met on horseback on the 6th of that month on the moor between Trailflat Kirk and Arthurstane in Dumfriesshire. Lord Maxwell was attended by Charles Maxwell of Kirkhouse, and Sir James Johnston by William Johnston of Locherby, Sir Robert Maxwell being also present. With Sir Robert Maxwell, the two chiefs rode apart to confer together, but a quarrel taking place between the attendants, Johnston's friend was shot at by a pistol fired by the other. The Laird of Johnston, crying out "treason" rode forward to see what was the matter. Lord Maxwell, at that moment, shot him in the back and he fell off his horse dead. After the murder of Johnston, his lordship immediately fled to the continent. His title and estates were forfeited, and all his offices vested in the crown.

In his absence, Maxwell was found guilty of three separate charges of treason and sentenced by Parliament on 24th June 1609 to loss of life, dignities, offices and lands for treasonable fire-raising and the slaughter of certain Johnstons at Dallebie in Nithsdale in 1602, for the breaking out of Edinburgh Castle in 1607, and the murder of the laird of Johnstone under trust in April 1608.

In March 1612 he ventured to return to Scotland, and being closely pursued, rode to Caithness, intending to take shipping there for Sweden. However, scandalously betrayed by his cousin the Fifth Earl of Caithness, Maxwell was captured near Caithness, taken to Castle Sinclair, and then by order of the Privy Council he was brought by sea to Leith and imprisoned for the third time in Edinburgh Castle on 19th September 1612. Maxwell confessed and craved mercy for his offence for the slaughter of Sir James Johnston. He offered to make amends, proposing to marry the late lairds daughter or to provide a dowry for his sister Lady Herries daughter if a marriage could be arranged between her and the young laird. He also suggested that he could be banished for 7 years.

One of the parties who refused to accept any settlement during his trial for the murder of Johnstone was the brother of his wife Margaret, the 2nd Marquis of Hamilton. Maxwell's proposals were all rejected.

John Maxwell was taken from the Tolbooth of Edinburgh to the Mercat Cross where on the scaffold he acknowledged that he justly deserved his punishment. He expressed his hope that the king would restore the family inheritance to his brother. He likewise 'asked forgiveness of the Laird of Johnston, his mother, grandmother, and friends, acknowledging the wrong and harm done to them, with protestation that it was without dishonour for the worldly part of it. 'Suffering his eyes to be covered with a handkerchief, he offered his head to the axe and suffered death the 21st May at 4 o'clock in the afternoon.'[2]

He was buried at Newbattle Abbey, Midlothian, Scotland, which was owned at the time by a distant relative.

---

2 Source - Pitcairns Criminal Trials, Volume 3, page 53.

Sir Walter Scott masterfully summarised the whole unhappy story in his Minstrelsy of the Scottish Borders;

> "Thus was finally ended, by a salutary example of severity, the 'foul debate' betwixt the Maxwells and the Johnstons, in the course of which each family lost two Chieftains; one dying of a broken heart, one in the field of battle, one by assassination, and one by the sword of the executioner."

Whoever the anonymous author of the story was, he or she had a good knowledge of the works of Scott for there are several direct references in 'The Battle of Dryffe Sands'. In 1802, Sir Walter Scott had published his first substantial work with ' The Minstrelsy of the Scottish Borders' which was a collection of historical and romantic ballads among which was one allegedly never before published 'Lord Maxwell's Goodnight'.

Another ballad included in the Minstrelsy was 'Armstrong's Goodnight' which was referred to in the original Tale as 'Johnnie Armstrong's Last Goodnight'. Declaring how John Armstrong and his Eightscore Men fought a bloody Battle with the Scotch King at Edenborough. To a pretty Northern Tune.

Thirdly, Scott included in the Minstrelsey 'The Feast of Spurs' by the Rev. John Marriott which was the story of one of Scotts ancestors …and his wife Mary Scott, the Flower of Yarrow. This told of Mary adopting the habit among Border wives to hint to her husband that he needed to go hunting, by presenting him with a dish containing a pair of clean spurs. This story features prominently in the Battle of Dryffe Sands.

Could the Battle of Dryffe Sands have been written by Scott himself? Sadly Scott died in 1832 four years before Wilson's Tale was published and surely such a coup would have been widely publicised. We will probably never know.

LORD MAXWELL'S GOODNIGHT

(Thought by Scott to have been written between 1608 and 1613). "Adieu, madame, my mother dear, But and my sister three! Adieu, fair Robert of Orchardstane! My heart is wae for thee. Adieu, my ladye, and only joy! For I may not stay with thee.

"Though I hae slain the Lord Johnstone, What care I for their feid: My noble mind their wrath disdains, - He was my father's deid. Both night and day I labour'd oft, Of him avenged to be; But now I've got what lang I sought, And I may not stay with thee.

"Adieu! Drumlanrig, false wert aye, And Closeburn in a band! The Laird of Lag, frae my father that fled, When the Johnstone struck off his hand. They were three brethren in a band - Joy may they never see! Their treacherous art, and cowardly heart, Hae twined my love and me.

"Adieu! Dumfries, my proper place, But and Carlaverock fair! Adieu! my castle of the Thrieve, Wi' a' my buildings there; Adieu! Lochmaben's gate sae fair, The Langholm-holm, where birks there be: Adieu! my ladye and only joy, For, trust me, I may not stay wi' thee.

"Adieu! fair Eskdale up and down, Where my puir friends do dwell; The bangisters will ding them down, And will them sair compell. But I'll avenge their feid mysell, When I come o'er the sea; Adieu! my layde, and only joy, For I may not stay wi' thee." -

"Lord of the land!" - that ladye said, "O wad ye go wi' me, Unto my brother's stately tower, Where safest ye may be! There Hamiltons, and Douglas baith, Shall rise to succour thee." - "Thanks for thy kindness, fair my dame, But I may not stay wi' thee." -

Then he tuik aff a gay gold ring, Thereat hang signets three; "Hae, tak thee that, mine ain dear thing, And still hae mind o' me: But if thou take another lord, Ere I come ower the sea - His life is but a three days' lease, Though I may not stay wi' thee." -

The wind was fair, the ship was clear, That good lord went away: And most part of his friends were there, To give him a fair convey. They drank the wine, they didna spair, Even in that gude lord's sight - Sae now he's o'er the floods sae gray, And Lord Maxwell has ta'en his Goodnight.

The River Dryfe

Lord Kames's Puzzle.

The Lawyer's Tales.

While looking over some Session papers which had belonged to Lord Kames I came across some fragmentary notes on the case of Napier versus Napier which his lordship referred to as one of the most curious puzzles that ever he had witnessed since he had taken his seat on the bench. I believe I have understood enough to set out the story and take the reader on a most unusual journey.

Imagine a small domicile in Toddrick's Wynd, in the old city of Edinburgh, the humble abode of a decent, hard-working washerwoman called Mrs. Hislop, and a young girl, verging upon sixteen, called Henrietta. Now she was as they say "as blithe as bonnie," and could have been the subject of countless tales and songs about pretty young damsels, but it is not her beauty as such which is of relevance to this tale, but certain unusual traits, namely a very slightest cast in the eyes, and a classic Roman nose, which she no more inherited from Mrs Hislop than her looks. These together with her generous and sympathetic nature endeared her to all whom she met, with one strange exception, for reasons which will become apparent.

So Mrs. Hislop was busy twisting into a serpent the sheets of Mr. Dallas, her employer and writer to the signet, sweating slightly and blushing like a peony. Suddenly Henney came rushing in, looking startled and excited.

"What think ye, minny?" she cried, as she held up her hands.

"The deil has risen again from the grave where he was buried in Kirkcaldy," was the reply, with a laugh.

"No, that's no it," continued the girl.

"Then what is it?" was the question.

"He's dead," replied Henney.

"Who is dead?" again asked Mrs. Hislop.

"The strange man," replied the girl.

Mrs Hislop paused in her work, and Henney, supposing that she was not understood, added--

"The man who used to look at me with yon terrible eyes."

"Yes, yes, dear, I understand you," said the woman, as she let the coil fall, and sat down upon a chair, under the influence of strong emotion. "But who told you?"

"Jean Graham," replied the girl.

The answer seemed, for certain reasons known to herself, to satisfy the woman, for never another word she said, and while Henny rushed off to tell her friends, she quietly and resolutely formulated a plan. This started with rising from her chair and taking from her blue chest her holiday suit, putting the humble fineries on, and heading off up the High Street.

Her destination was the writing-booth of Mr. James Dallas, writer to his Majesty's Signet. The gentleman was minutely scanning some papers hunting for "flaws", a species of game that is both a prey and a reward. He was not altogether pleased to be interrupted by the entrance of Mrs Margaret Hislop of Toddrick's Wynd, though he soon realised that she had not come as his washerwoman, but as a client, as she drew up a chair opposite him and hitching her round body into something like stiff dignity, seated herself. Nor was this change from her usual deportment the only one she underwent, for as soon appeared, her style of speech was to pass from broad Scotch, not altogether into the

"Inglis" of the upper ranks, but into a mixture of the two tongues; a feat which she performed remarkably well.

"And so Mr. Napier of Eastleys is dead?" she began.

"Yes," answered the writer, perhaps with a portion of cheerfulness, seeing he was that gentleman's agent, or "doer," as it was then called; a word far more expressive, as many clients can testify, at least after they are "done;" and seeing also that a dead client is not finally "done" until his affairs are wound up and consigned to the green box.

"And wha is his heir, think ye?" continued his questioner.

"Why, Charles Napier, his nephew," answered the writer, somewhat carelessly.

"I'm no just a'thegither sure of that, Mr. Dallas," said she, with another effort at dignity, which was unfortunately qualified by a knowing wink.

"The deil's in the woman," was the sharp retort, as the writer opened his eyes wider than he had done since he laid down his parchments.

"Maybe," said she; "but this I'm sure of, that Henrietta Hislop--that's our Henney, ye ken--the brawest and bonniest lass in Toddrick's Wynd is the lawful heiress of Mr. John Napier, and was called Henrietta after her mother."

"The honest woman's red wud," said the writer, laughing. "Why, Mrs. Hislop, I always took you for a shrewd, sensible woman. Do you really think that, because you bore a child to Mr. John Napier, therefore Henney Hislop is the heiress of her reputed father?"

"Me bear a bairn to Mr. Napier!" cried the offended client. "Wha ever said I was the mother of Henney Hislop?"

"Everybody," replied he. "We never doubted it, though I admit she has none of your features."

"Everybody is a leear, then," rejoined the woman tartly. "There's no a drap of blood in the lassie's body can claim kindred with me or mine."

"And whose daughter, by the mother's side, is she, then?" asked he, as his curiosity began to wax stronger.

"Ay, you have now your hand on the cocked egg," replied she, with a look of mystery. "The other was a wind ane, and you've just to sit a little and you'll see the chick."

The writer settled himself into attention, and the good dame thought it proper, like some preachers who pause two or three minutes (the best part of their discourse) after they have given out the text, to retain her speech until she had attained the due solemnity.

She began in a low mysterious voice, " Sixteen years ago come June, about eleven o'clock at night on the fifteenth as I was making ready for my bed I heard a knock at my door, and the words of a woman, 'Oh, Mrs. Hislop, Mrs. Hislop!' So I ran and opened the door; and wha think ye I saw but Jean Graham, Mr. Napier's cook, with een like twa candles, and her mouth as wide as if she had been to swallow the biggest sup of porridge that ever crossed ploughman's craig?"

"'What's ado, woman?' said I, for I thought something fearful had happened.

"'Oh,' cried she, 'my lady's lighter, and ye're to come to Meggat's Land, this minute, and bide nae man's hindrance.'

"'And so I will,' said I, as I threw my red plaid ower my head, and out we came, jolting each other in the dark through sheer hurry and confusion, down the Canongate to Meggat's Land, in at the kitchen door, through to a back room. When my eyes adjusted to the light I saw a man and Mrs. Kemp the howdie busy rowing something in flannel.

"'Get along,' said the man to Jean; 'you're not wanted here.'

"And as Jean made off, Mrs. Kemp turned to me--

"'Come here, Mrs. Hislop,' said she.

"So I slipt forward; but the never a word more was said for ten minutes, they were so intent on getting the bairn all right. For ye ken, sir, it was a new-born babe they were busy with. It was so quiet I could hear their breathing, and when they had finished:

"'Mrs. Hislop,' said the man, as he turned to me, 'you're to take this child and bring it up as your own, or anybody else's you like, except Mr. Napier's, and you're never to say when or how you got it, for it's a banned creature, with the curse upon it of a malison for the sins of him who begot it and of her who bore it. Swear to it.' and he held up his hand.

"And I swore; but I thought I would just take the advice of the Lord how far my words would bind me to do evil, or leave me to do gude, when the time came. So I took the bairn into my arms.

"'And wha will pay for the wet-nurse?' said I; 'for ye ken I am as dry as a yeld crummie. This is all I ask.'

"'I was coming to that,' said he, 'if your supple tongue had left you power to hear mine. In this leathern purse there are twenty gowden guineas, a goodly sum, and never a penny more you may expect, for all connection between this child and this house or its master is to be from this moment finished for ever.'

"And a gude quittance it was, I thought, with a bonny bairn and twenty guineas on my side, and nothing on the other but maybe a father's anger and salt tears, besides the wrath of God against those who forsake their children. So with thankfulness enough I carried away my bundle; and ye'll guess that Henney Hislop is now the young woman of fifteen who was then that child of a day."

"And is this all the evidence," said the writer, "you have to prove that Henrietta Hislop is the daughter of Mr. and Mrs. Napier?"

"Maybe no," replied she; "if ye weren't so like the English stranger wha curst the Scotch kail because he did not see on the table the beef that was coming from the kitchen, besides the haggis and the bread-pudding. You've only as yet got the broth, and, for the rest, I will give you Mrs. Kemp, wha told me, as a secret, that the child was brought into the world by her own hands from the living body of Mrs. Napier. Will that satisfy you?"

"No," replied Mr. Dallas, who had got deeper and deeper into a study. "Mr. Napier, I know, was at home that evening when his wife bore a child. That child never could have been given away without his consent, and as for the consent itself, it is a still greater improbability, seeing that he was always anxious for an heir to Eastleys."

"And so maybe he was," replied she; "but I see you are only at the beef yet, and you may be better pleased when you have got the haggis, let alone the pudding. Yea, it is even likely Mr. Napier wanted an heir, and, what is more, he got one, at least an heiress; but sometimes God gives and the devil misgives. And so it was here; for Mr. Napier took it into his head that the child was not his, and, in place of being pleased with an heir, he thought himself cursed with a bastard, begotten on his wife by no other than Captain Preston, his lady's cousin. And where did the devil find that poison growing but in the heart of Isabel Napier, the sister of that very Charles who is now thinking he will heir Eastleys by pushing aside poor Henney? And then the poison, like the old apple, was so fair and tempting. For Mr. Napier had been married ten years, and enjoyed the love that is so bonnie a 'little while when it is new,' and yet had no children, till this one came so exactly nine months after the captain's visit to Scotland. So Satan had little more to do than hold up the temptation. You see, sir, how things come round. Mrs. Napier died next day after the birth. Mr. Napier lived a miserable man. Henney was brought up in poverty, and sometimes distress, but now I hope she has come to her kingdom."

Here Mrs. Hislop stopped, and as there could be no better winding-up of a romance than by bringing her heroine to her kingdom at last, she felt well pleased with her conclusion, but the writer, rather than accepting her proofs, lay back in his chair in a deep reverie, before fixing his eyes upon her with a look of scepticism.

"Mrs. Hislop," said he, "if it had not been that I have always taken you for an honest woman, I would say that you are art and part in fabricating a story without a particle of foundation. There may possibly be some mystery about the birth and parentage of the young girl. You may have got her out of the house of Meggat's Land in the Canongate from a man, not Mr. Napier, you admit, who may have been the father of it by some mother residing in the house; and Mrs. Kemp may have been actuated, by some unknown means, to remove the paternity from the right to the wrong person. All this is possible, but that the child could be that one which Mrs. Napier bore is impossible for this reason, and I beg of you to listen to it, that Mrs. Napier's child was dead-born and according to good evidence buried in the same coffin with the mother."

A statement this, which, delivered in the solemn manner of an attorney who was really honest, and who knew much of this history, appeared to Mrs. Hislop so strange that her tongue was paralyzed, an effect which had never before been produced by any one of all the five causes of the metaphysicians. Even her eyes seemed to have lost their power of movement, and as for her wits, they had, like those of the renowned

Astolpho, surely left and taken refuge in the moon.

"If you are not satisfied with my words," continued the writer (no doubt ironically, for where could he have found better evidence of the effect of his statement?), "I will give you writing for the truth of what I have said to you."

And rising and going towards a green tin box, he opened the same, and taking therefrom a piece of paper, he resumed his seat.

"Now listen," said he, as he unfolded an old yellow-coloured sheet of paper, and then he read these words: "'Your presence is requested at the funeral of Henrietta Preston, my wife, and of a child still-born, from my house, Meggat's Land, Canongate, to the burying-ground at St. Cuthberts, on Friday the 19th of this month June, at one o'clock.' The name at this letter," continued Mr. Dallas, "is that of 'John Napier of Eastleys.' Will that satisfy you?"

And the "doer" for Mr. Charles Napier, conceiving that he had at last effectually "done" his client's opponent, seemed well pleased to sit and witness the further effect of his evidence on the bewildered woman; but she recovered the powers of both her eyes and her tongue in much less time than the writer expected, and in a manner, too, very different from that for which he was probably prepared.

"Weel," replied she, smiling, "it would just seem that even the haggis has not pleased you, Mr. Dallas" and putting her hand into a big side-pocket she extracted a small piece of paper. She continued: "But ye see a guid, honest Scotchwoman's no to be suspected of being shabby at her own table. So read ye that, which you may take for the bread-pudding."

And the writer, having taken the paper, held it before his face for a long a time until he turned a look upon the woman of dark suspicion--

"Where, in God's name, got you this?" he said.

"Just read it out first," replied she. "Ye read yer ain paper, and why no mine?"

And the writer read, perhaps more easily than he could understand, the strange words:

"This child, born of my wife, and yet neither of my blood nor my lineage, I repudiate, and, unable to push it back into the dark world of nothing from which it came, I leave it with a scowl to the mercy which countervaileth the terrible decree whereby the sins of the parent shall be visited on the child. This I do on the 15th of June 17. JOHN NAPIER of Eastleys, in the county of Mid-Lothian."

After reading this extraordinary denunciation, Mr. Dallas sat and considered, as if at a loss what to say, but whether it was that scepticism was at the root of his thoughts, or that he assumed it as a mask to conceal misgivings to which he did not like to confess, he put a question:

"Where got you this notable piece of evidence?"

"Ay," replied Mrs. Hislop, "you are getting reasonable on the last dish. That bit of paper, which to me and my dear Henney is werth the haill estate of Eastleys, was found by me carefully pinned to the flannel in which the child was wrapt."

"Wonderful enough surely," repeated he, "if true", the latter words being pronounced with emphasis which made the rough liquid letter sound like a hurling stone. "But," he continued, "the whole document, in its terms of crimination and exposure, and not less the wild manner of its application, is so unlike the act of a man not absolutely frantic, that I cannot believe it to be genuine."

"But you know, Mr. Dallas," replied she, "that Mr. John Napier was a man who, if he threw a stone, cared little whether it struck the kirk window or the mill door."

"That is so far true, but, passionate and unforgiving as he was, he was not so reckless as to be regardless whether the stone did not come back on his own head."

"And it's no genuine!" she resumed, as, disregarding his latter words, she relapsed into her more familiar dialect. "The Lord help ye! canna ye look at first the ae paper and then the ither? and if they're no alike, mustna the ither be the forgery?"

An example of the conditional syllogism which might have amused even a writer to the signet, if he had not been at the very moment busy in the examination of the handwriting of the funeral letter and that of the paper of repudiation and malison. The resemblance, or rather the identity of which was so striking, as to reduce all his theories to confusion.

"By all that's good in heaven, the same," he muttered to himself; and then addressing his visitor, "I confess, Mrs. Hislop," said he, "that this paper has driven me somewhat off my point of confidence. But I suppose you will see that, if the child was actually, as the letter indicates, buried with its mother, Henrietta's rights are at an end. It

is just possible, however, I fairly admit, that Mr. Napier, who was a very eccentric man, may have so worded the letter as to induce the world to believe that the so-considered illegitimate child had been dead-born, while he gratified, privately he might verily think, his vengeance by writing this terrible curse. Still I think you are wrong, but as this wonderful paper gives you a plausible plea, I would recommend you to Mr. White in Mill's Court, who will see to the young woman's rights. He will be the flint, and I the steel, and between our friendly opposition we will produce a spark which will light up the candle of truth."

"Ay," replied she; "only as the spark of fire comes from the steel, we'll just suppose you are the flint and by my troth you're hard enough; but, come as it may, it will light the lantern that will show Henney Napier to the bonnie haughs of Eastleys."

Mrs. Hislop having got back her paper from Mr. Dallas, left the writer's chambers, and directed her steps to Mill's Court, where she found Mr. White busy poring over law papers. She was, as we have seen, one of those few women who can make their own introduction acceptable, and moreover tell a story that will secure the attention of a busy listener. So Mr. White heard her narrative, not only with interest, but even a touch of the pervading sympathy of the spirit of romance. And so he might, for who doesn't see that the charm of mystery can be enhanced by the hope of turning it to account of money? Wherefore he began to interrogate his client as to who could speak to the doings in the house in Meggat's Land on that eventful night when the child was born, and having taken notes of the answers, he paused a little, as if to consider what was the first step he ought to take into the region of doubt, and perhaps of intrigue, where at least there must be lies floating about like films in the clear atmosphere of truth. Nor had he meditated many minutes till he rose, and taking up his square hat and his gold-headed cane, he said:

"Come, we will try what we can discover in a quarter where an end of the ravelled string ought to be found, whether complicated into a knot by the twisting power of self-interest or no."

And leading the way, he proceeded with his client down the High Street until they came to the Canongate Tolbooth, where out from a dark entry sprang a young woman, who bounding forward seized our good dame round the neck. This was no other than Henney Hislop herself, who, though dressed in the humblest garb had an air of grace and her handsome features, if you abated the foresaid cast or slight squint in the eyes, suggested she could have been a Napier even if she wasn't. A few words whispered in Mrs. Hislop's ear, and the girl was off, leaving our couple to proceed on their way. Even this incident had its use, for Mr. White, who had known Mr. Napier, and had faith in the hereditary descent of bodily aspects, could not restrain himself from the remark, however much it might inflame the hopes of his client:

"The curse has left no blight there," said he. "That is the very face of Mr. Napier--the high nose especially, and as for the eyes, with that unmistakeable cast, why, I have seen their foretypes in the head of John Napier a hundred times."

An observation so congenial to Mrs. Hislop, that she could not help being a little humorous, even in the depth of an anxiety which had kept her silent for the full space of ten minutes.

"Nose, sir! there wasn't a man frae the castle yett to Holyrood wha could have produced that nose except John Napier."

And without further interruption than her own laugh, they proceeded till they came to the entry called Big Lochend Close. As they made their way in they encountered a woman in a plaid with a lantern in her hand. Though her face was illuminated by a gleam from the light she gave them little opportunity for examination, hurrying away as if she had been afraid of being searched for stolen property.

"Isbel Napier," whispered Mrs. Hislop, "she wha first brought evil into the house of the Napiers, with all its woe."

"And who bodes us small hope here," said he, "if she has been with the nurse."

And entering the room from which the ill-omening woman had issued, they found another, sitting by the fire, torpid and corpulent, to a degree which indicated that as it had been her trade to nurse others, she had not forgotten herself in her ministrations.

"Mrs. Temple," said Mr. White, who saw the policy of speaking fair the woman who had been so recently in the company of an evil genius; "I am glad to find you so stout and hearty."

"Neither o' the twa, sir," replied she; "for I am rather weak and heartless. Many a ane I hae nursed into health and strength, but a' nursing comes hame in the end."

"And some, no doubt, have died under your care," continued the writer, with a view to introduce his subject; "and therefore you should be grateful for the life that is still spared to you. You could not save the life of Mrs. Napier."

"That's an auld story, and a waefu' ane," she replied, with a side-look at Mrs. Hislop, "and I hae nae heart to mind it. Some said the lady wasna innocent, and doubtless Mr. Napier thought sae, for he took high dealings wi' her, and looked at her wi' a scorn that would have scathed whinstanes. Sae it was better she was ta'en awa--ay, and her baby wi' her. For if it had lived, it would have dree'd the revenge o' that stern man."

"The child!" said Mr. White, "did it die too?"

"Dee! ye may rather ask if it ever lived; for it never drew breath, in this world at least."

A statement so strange, that it brought the eyes of the two visitors to each other, and no doubt both of them recurred in memory to the statement in the funeral letter which, whatever may have been the case with the assertion now made by the nurse, never could have been dictated by her they had met in the passage, and no doubt they both remembered the statement made by Mr. Dallas, to the effect that both the mother and child were buried together.

"Never drew breath, you say, nurse!" resumed Mr. White, with an air of astonishment. "Why I have been given to understand not only that the child was born alive, but that it is actually living now."

"Weel," replied the nurse, "maybe St. Cuthbert has wrought a miracle, and brought the child out o' the grave by the West Church; but he has wrought nae miracle on me, to mak' me forget what my een saw, and my hands did, that day when I helped to place the dead body o' the innocent on the breast o' its dead mother. Ay, and bent her stiff arms sae as to bring them ower her bairn, just as if she had been faulding it to her bosom. And sae in this fashion were they buried."

"And you would swear to that, Mrs. Temple?" said the writer.

"Ay, upon fifty Bibles, ane after anither," was the reply, in something like a tone of triumph.

Nor could the woman be induced to swerve from these assertions, notwithstanding repeated interrogations; and the writer was left to the conclusion, which he preferred, rather than place any confidence in the funeral letter, that the nurse's statement was in some mysterious way connected with the visit of Isabel Napier. It was not so very mysterious after all, when we are to consider that her brother was preparing to claim Eastleys, as well as the valuable furniture of the house in Meggat's Land, as the nearest lawful heir of his deceased uncle.

But their inquiries were not finished. Retracing their steps up the Canongate they landed in the Fountain Close, where, under the leading of Mrs. Hislop, the writer was procured another witness, and this was no other than that same Jean Graham, who was sent to Toddrick's Wynd on that eventful night, fifteen years before, to bring Mrs. Hislop to the house in Meggat's Land. She was one of those simple souls, of which we wish there were more in the world, who look upon a lie as rather an operose affair, and who seem to be truthful from sheer laziness. There was accordingly no difficulty here, for the woman rolled off her story just as if it had been coiled up in her mind for all that length of time.

"There was a terrible stir in the house that night," she began. "The nurse, wha is yet living in Lochend Close, and Mrs. Kemp the howdie, wha is dead, were wi' my lady, and John Cowie, the butler, was busy attending our master, who had been the haill day in ane o' his dark fits. Then I was sent for you, and brought you, and you'll mind how Cowie bade me go along. But I listened at the door, and heard what the butler said to ye when he gied ye the bairn, and think ye I didna see ye carry it along the passage as ye left? Sae far I could understand, but when I heard Mrs. Kemp say the bairn was still-born, and Cowie declare it was better it was dead and awa, I couldna comprehend this. Nor do I weel yet, but we just thought that as there was something wrang between master and my lady, he wanted us to believe that the bairn was dead, for very shame o' being thought the father, when maybe he wasna. And then he was so guid to me and my neighbour Anne Dickson, ye mind o' her, puir soul, she's dead too, that we couldna, for the very heart o' us, say a word o' what we knew. But now when Mr. Napier is dead, and the brother o' that wicked Jezebel, Isbel Napier, may try to take the property frae Henney, wha I aye kenned as a Napier, with the very nose and een o' the father, I have spoken out, and may the Lord gie the right to whom the right is due!"

"It's all right," said the writer, after he had jotted with a pencil the evidence of Jean, as well as that of the nurse; "and if we could find this John Cowie, we might so fortify the orphan's rights, as to defy Miss Napier and her brother and Mr. Dallas and all the witnesses they can bring."

"Ay," continued the woman, "but I doubt if you'll catch him. He left Mr. Napier's service about ten years ago, and I never heard mair o' him."

"Nor I either," said Mrs. Hislop.

"Well, we must search for him," added Mr. White; "for that man alone, so far as I can see, is he who will unravel this strange business."

And thus the day's work finished. Mrs. Hislop sought her humble dwelling and Henney, though she didn't utter a word about the days business that might betray her doubts, hopes, and anxieties.

Meanwhile the agent was in his own house, revolving all the points of a most curious puzzle. Sometimes he felt confidence, and at other times despair, and of course he had the consolation that the opposite party was undergoing the same process of oscillation. It was clear enough that Cowie was the required Oedipus, and if it should turn out that he was dead, or could not be found, the advantage was on the part of Charles Napier, insomuch as, while he was indisputably the nephew of the deceased, the orphan, Henrietta, was under the necessity of proving her birth and pedigree.

And so, as it appeared, Mr. Dallas was of that opinion, for the very next day he applied to Chancery for a writ to get Charles Napier served nearest and lawful heir to his uncle. And as in legal warfare there is small room for retiring tactics, Mr. White felt himself obliged, however anxious he was to gain time, to follow his opponent's example by taking out a competing writ in favour of Henrietta.

The parties were now face to face in court, and the battle behoved to be fought out. But as in all legal cases, where the circumstances are strange or peculiar, the story soon gets wind, so here the Meggat's Land romance was by-and-by all over the city. It was a favourite opinion of some that the case could only be cleared by supposing that a dead stranger child had been surreptitiously passed off, and even coffined, as the true one, while others, equally skilled in the art of divining, maintained that the child given to Mrs. Hislop by Cowie was a bastard of his own, by the terrible woman Isabel Napier, who was thus, according to the ordinary working of public prejudice, raised to a height of crime sufficient to justify the hatred of the people. On which presumption, it behoved to be assumed that the paper containing the curse was a forgery by Cowie and his associate in crime, and that the money paid to Mrs. Hislop was furnished by the lady. All which suppositions, and others not less incredible, were greedily accepted for the very reason that it required something prodigious to explain an enigma which exhausted the ordinary sources of man's ingenuity.

But all these suppositions were destined to undergo refractions through the medium of a new fact. The case, by technical processes, came before the Court of Session, where the diversity of opinion was, proportionably to the number of judges, as great as among the quidnuncs outside. The only clear idea in the heads of the robed and wigged wiseacres was, that the case, Napier versus Napier, was a puzzle which no man could read or solve. That was until Lord Kames suggested the possibility of getting an additional piece of evidence through the examination of the coffin wherein Mrs. Napier was buried. Accordingly a commission was issued to one of the Faculty to proceed to the West Church burying-ground, and there cause to be laid open and examined the coffin of the said Mrs. Henrietta Preston or Napier, with the view to ascertain whether or not the body of a child had been placed therein along with the corpse of the mother.

This commission was accordingly executed, and the report bore, that "he, the commissioner did find the skeletons of two bodies in the said coffin identified as that of the said lady, one whereof was that of a woman apparently of middle age, and the other that of a babe, which lay upon the chest of the larger skeleton held in that position by the arms of the same being laid across it; that having satisfied himself of these facts, the commissioner accordingly made this report to their lordships."

The fact thus ascertained the case was again put to the Roll for a hearing on the effect of the new evidence. It was contended for the nephew by Mr. Wight that the question was now virtually settled, insomuch that the court was not bound to solve riddles, but to find to whom pertained a certain right of inheritance. The birth of the child had been sworn to by the nurse, as well as its death, and the final peculiar placing of it in the coffin, which the court now had proof of from their own commissioner. All claim on the part of the girl was thus virtually excluded, for the proceedings which took place that evening in another room, under circumstances of suspicion, were sworn to only by Mrs. Hislop herself, an interested witness, and were only partially confirmed by an eavesdropper. These suspicious proceedings might be explained by as many hypotheses as had been devised by the wise judges of the taverns, among which was the theory of the living child being Cowie's own by Isabel Napier, and palmed off as Mrs. Napier's to hide the shame of the true mother. All unlikely enough, no doubt, but not so impossible as that the coffined child should now be alive and awaiting the issue of this case, in the expectation of being Lady of Eastleys.

On the other side, Mr. Andrews, counsel for Henrietta, maintained that while his learned brother assumed the one half of the case as proved, and repudiated the other as a lie or a myth, he had a right to embrace the other half, and pronounce the first a stratagem or trick. The proceedings in the back-room into which Jean Graham introduced Mrs. Hislop were more completely substantiated than those in the bedroom where Mrs. Napier lay. For while the one were sworn to by Mrs. Hislop herself, a soothfast witness, and confirmed in all points by the woman Graham, the other were attempted to be proven by the solitary testimony of the nurse Temple. The paper containing the curse was as indisputably in the handwriting of Mr. Napier as was the funeral letter. The money paid was proved by the fact that the orphan had been kept and educated for fifteen years. The name Henrietta was not likely to have been a mere coincidence, and it was still more unlikely that a respectable woman such as Mrs. Hislop would invent a story of affiliation so strangely in harmony with the secrets of the house in Meggat's Land, and fortify it by a forged document. Then Mrs. Hislop was unable to write, and no attempt had been made on the other side to prove that Henrietta had a father other than he who was pointed out by the paper of the curse. So he (the counsel) might follow the example of his brother, and hold the other half of the case to be unexplainable by hypotheses, however ridiculous. The child having been disposed of to Mrs. Hislop, a fact thus proved, what was to prevent him (the counsel) from going also to the haunts of the taverns for the theory that Mr. Napier, or some plotter for him in the shape of Mrs. Kemp or John Cowie, substituted the dead child of a stranger for the living one of his wife, and bribed the nurse Temple to tell the tale she had told? To which she would be more inclined by the golden promptings of the woman Isabel Napier, the niece, whose brother would, in the event of the stratagem being concealed, succeed to the estate of Eastleys.

At the conclusion of these pleadings, just as the judges thought they had seen their way to a judgment against the orphan, Mr. Andrews rose and made a statement, perhaps as fictitious as a counsel's conscience would permit, to the effect that the agent (Mr. White) had procured some trace of the butler Cowie, who could throw more light on the case than Death had done, and that if some time were accorded to complete the inquiry, something might turn up which would alter the complexion even of this Protean mystery. The request was granted.

But, in truth, Mr. Andrews' suggestion was simply a bit of ingenuity, intended to ward off an unfavourable judgment, and allow a development of the chapter of accidents. No trace had yet been got of Cowie. It was not even known whether he was alive. But if we allow fate some fourteen days to write a new chapter we may come to a day whereupon a certain person, in an inn far down in a valley of Westmoreland, in the little town called Kirby Lonsdale, was busy reading the Caledonian Mercury. It was certainly no wonder that the paper should contain an account of the romance wrapped up in the case Napier versus Napier. And we would have set him down as one given to the reading of riddles, for after he had perused the paragraph he looked as if he knew more about that case than anyone else. Nor was he contented with an indication of a mere look of wisdom: he actually burst out into a laugh, an expression wondrously unsuited to the gravity of the subject. The reader of the Mercury was verily Mr. John Cowie, whilom butler to Mr. John Napier, and now waiter in the Lonsdale Arms of the obscure Kirby, a place like Peebles, where if you wanted to deposit a secret you could do so by crying it out at the market-cross. Moreover, he was verily in possession of the key to the Napier mystery.

Accordingly Mr. White of Mill's Court two days afterwards received a letter informing him that John Cowie was the writer of the same, and that, if a reasonable consideration were held out to him, he would proceed to the northern metropolis, and there settle for ever a case which apparently had kept the newsmongers of Edinburgh in aliment much exceeding the normal nine days. Mr. White saw the danger of promising anything which could be construed into a reward, but he could use other means of decoying the shy bird into his meshes. These he used in his answer with such effect that the man who could solve the mystery was in Edinburgh at the end of a week. Nor was Mr. White unprepared to receive him, for he had previously got a commission to examine him and take his deposition. But then an agent likes to know what a witness will say before he cites him, and the canny Scotchman, of all men in the world, is the most uncanny if brought to swear without some hope of being benefited by his oath. There was, therefore, need of tact as well as delicacy, and Mr. White contrived in the first place to get his man to take up his quarters in the house in Mill's Court. A good supper and chambers formed the first demulcent,we do not say bribe, because by a legal fiction all eating and drinking is set down to the score of hospitality. A Scotch breakfast followed in the morning, at which were present Mrs. White and Mrs. Hislop, and our favourite Henney, the last of whom, spite of all the efforts of her putative mother to keep from her the secret of her birth and prospects, had caught the infection of the general topic of the city, and wondered at her strange fortune. No man can precognosce like a woman, and here were three, but perhaps they might have all failed, had it not been for the natural art of Henney, who out of pure goodness and gratitude, was so delighted with the man who had rolled her in a blanket and sent her to her beloved mother, as she still called her, that she promised to make him butler at Eastleys, and keep him comfortable all his days.

"Now," said the cautious agent, "this promise of Henney's is not made in consideration of your giving evidence for her before the commissioner."

"I'm thinking of nothing but her face," said John. "I could swear to it out of a thousand, and Heaven bless her for I think I am again in the once happy house in Meggat's Land."

And John pretended he was wiping a morsel of egg from his mouth, while the handkerchief was extended as far as the eye.

"A terrible night that was," he continued. "Mrs. Napier had been in labour all day and when Mrs. Kemp told me to tell my master that my lady had been delivered of TWINS"

"Twins!" cried they all, as if moved by some sympathetic chord which ran from heart to heart.

"Ay, twins," he repeated; "one dead, and another living, even you yourself, Henney, who are as like your father as if there never had been a Captain Preston in the world."

And thus was John Cowie precognosced. We need not say that he was that very day examined before the commissioner. He gave an account of all the proceedings of the house in Meggat's Land on the eventful night to which we have referred. The case was no longer a puzzle and accordingly a decision was given in favour of Henrietta, whereby we have one other example of truth and right emerging from darkness into light. Some time afterwards, the heiress, with Mrs. Hislop alongside, and John Cowie on the driver's box, proceeded to Eastleys and took possession. There Henrietta acted the part of a generous lady, Mrs. Hislop that of a kind of a dowager, and John was once more butler in the house of the Napiers.

We stop here. Those who feel interest enough in the fortunes of Henney to inquire when and whom she married, and what were the subsequent fortunes of a life so strangely begun, will do well to go to Eastleys.

Retold by Michael Scott-Watson

Lord Kames Puzzle companion piece

Lord Kames – a beacon of the Enlightenment

To find Lord Kames featured in Wilson's Tales comes as no great surprise. This particular Tale was written by Alexander Leighton – who as well editing the Tales after Wilson's death contributed many of them. One can see both Leighton and Wilson admiring and perhaps being a little jealous of the career Kames forged for himself.

Lord Kames, as he became, was born Henry Home in 1696: the son of a modest laird who resided at Kames House, Berwickshire. He became one of the key figures in the Scottish Age of Enlightenment. A man for all seasons, he was renowned as a writer, philosopher, advocate and judge – and played a key role in the development and improvement of both agriculture and the Scottish linen industry.

While not from a poor background, he was not part of the aristocracy either. Educated modestly by the local minister, he moved to Edinburgh to pursue a career as a 'writer', or solicitor.

In reality, that involved a lot of clerking and copying for lawyers. This led to an encounter with Lord President Dalrymple when delivering documents to him at home. He left several hours later so impressed by the life of learned ease and dignity enjoyed by senior members of the legal profession that he resolved to become one of them.

At that time the profession was dominated by the aristocracy. Admission would normally involve time at university and often a stint studying abroad; but Home had to educate himself. It is reported that the struggles at this stage of his life became bitter memories in his years of prosperity.

He would often say that he would not have put himself through such drudgery of mind and body if he'd had an assured income of £50 a year. For want of which, he toiled through the ranks – becoming an advocate in 1723 and taking the title Lord Kames on appointment as a judge in 1752. This brought him £500 a year.

In his 1908 book Scottish Men of Letters in the Eighteenth Century, Henry Grey Graham gives this account of Kames' style on the bench: "With caustic temper and flurrying manner, he bullied dull judges out of their dignity, worried witnesses out of their memories, and nagged pleaders out of their arguments". One frustrated counsel complained that "he has the obstinacy of a mule and the levity of a harlequin".

Such a style no doubt put a few backs up along the way. But he won the praise and delight of the Scottish legal profession with his publication in 1741 of two vast folios of his Dictionary of Decisions of the Court of Session: the first systematic and orderly summary of Scots case law and precedent. The legal profession would be eternally grateful for this effort, as before this they'd had to rely on living memory and much searching of dusty papers.

I have so far found no evidence that the case of Napier v Napier actually happened. But I did encounter an interesting English case of the same name from 1915, considering whether refusal to allow marital intercourse nullified a marriage. Wilson's Tales research can take you down some surprising rabbit holes!

Kames did preside over one famous case which resonates with today's sensitivities. This concerned the matter of whether a slave, Joseph Knight, could still be regarded as his master's slave once brought back from the colonies to Scotland. Kames ruled that, as slavery was not legal in Scotland, Knight could not be regarded or treated as a slave once there. This was an enlightened decision, given that Scotland still had its own form of slavery legally enshrined in acts of 1606 and 1775. These laws, not abolished till 1799, required colliers and salters who were bonded to landowners from birth to live at and work the mines of their masters.

Kames had a commercial eye and was an original proprietor and backer of the British Linen Company, which he saw as a way of helping Scotland prosper.

He was also a founding member of the Philosophical Society of Edinburgh. This body's main purpose was to discuss philosophy – embracing a wide range of sciences – over ale, claret and oysters. It all sounds very enjoyable.

Kames was no laggard in his contribution to such debates and his literary output continued. His Historical Law Tracts set out his views on a four-stage evolution of society from hunter-gatherers to herders of animals, then agriculturalists developing specialist skills to cultivate land and needing laws to govern their activities. The final stage was commercial society, developing towns, ports and infrastructure to support trade – requiring further specialisation and of course more laws!

1761 saw the publication of an Introduction to the Art of Thinking. This was followed in 1762 by Elements of Criticism, which set out rules for literary composition and sought to discuss what constituted and defined beauty.

Sketches of the History of Man followed in 1774, somewhat predating Darwin's 1859 Origin of Species and advancing the view that God had created races from different stock in different parts of the world.

Kames had previously found himself in trouble with the church over his writings. His 1751 Essays on the Principles of Moral and Natural Religion, though intended to defend religion, were seen rather differently by some members of the clergy. He was charged with infidelity and the matter was debated before the General Assembly of the Church of Scotland, which issued a solemn exhortation against the proliferation of pernicious infidel books.

Kames was undeterred. He wrote tirelessly – some said to the neglect of his legal duties – while also taking a great interest in what others were publishing. He would enter into correspondence with authors on any subject or opinion that caught his eye, so eagerly that some became overwhelmed and simply stopped replying.

His output was so prolific that when he asked Lord Monboddo if he had read his latest book, Monboddo replied: "No my Lord, you write a great deal faster than I am able to read!" They were rivals, and Monboddo rarely missed an opportunity to put Kames down and mock his lower-class origins.

In 1776 he married Agatha Drummond, who inherited Blair Drummond near Stirling – now perhaps best known as the home of Scotland's leading safari park. Much of this inheritance was deep bog. Kames could see its potential if the peat was cleared and the land drained; so he set about cutting ditches, clearing peat and introducing waterwheels to shift the water. He offered tenancies to those willing to come and do the work on the basis that they could live rent-free for the first seven years. When he died in 1782, the area supported 29 tenants and their families. By the 1811 census 740 people were living in the area, and the whole process continued until 1840.

The drainage programme also opened-up access to the Highlands, which had previously only really been accessible via narrow routes through and round the endless bogs.

In 1776, at the age of 80, Kames set out his experiences in a monumental 400-page book: Gentleman Farmer; Being an Attempt to Improve Agriculture by Subjecting it to the Test of Rational Principles. He also called for the creation of a Board of Agriculture to drive more widespread improvement of agricultural practices.

He seems to have been remarkably active and alert in his later years, asking: "Why should I sit with my finger in my cheek waiting till death takes me?" His friend Mrs Montagu stated in her memoirs that "at 84 he is as gay and as nimble as when he was 25, his sight, hearing, memory perfect; he is a most entertaining companion".

When he died, aged 86, he was acknowledged as a leading light of the Enlightenment. Adam Smith, hearing an Englishman praise Scotland's intellectual elite, responded: "Yes, but we must every one of us acknowledge Lord Kames as our master".

Lord Kames' Puzzle was one of the first tales to be dramatised for the Wilson's Tales Project, set in the style of a radio play by local playwright Robert Wilkinson. It was wonderfully presented by the Berwick Broadcasting Company at Paxton House in 2013.

Background by Andrew Ayre

Small Tales...

...and perhaps a cheeky one...

...or, a humorous one...

You may have seen that the Wilson's Tales Project began a lighthearted aside in the shape of a 'challenge' to produce a Tale in 100 words.

It all started at a Wilson Memorial Dinner, as a bit of fun. Who knew that the entire Tale of The Vacant Chair (the very first Tale) could be mophed into 100 words? it took Wilson 5,000, and didn't have a humorous ending

The results were varied, readable, entertaining, so we're asking for more.

There are no limits on subject, era, or location. All genres welcome. Usual strictures about decorum of course. Current affairs and political satire is OK - but be aware that it ages.

The only requirement is that it has a beginning and end, and that it is exactly 100 words, not including the title.

Come on - everybody has 100 words lying around unused, and you can use them in almost any order.. No time limits - this is ongoing.

Single or multiple submissions to - WilsonsTales@gmail.com

The Vacant Chair

Poor Tom Elliot.

Snatched by smugglers on his 18th birthday. Enslaved on a Dutch man o'war. Forced to fight the English, then the French, who took him prisoner. Finally escaped - now aged 30.

Battled his way back, to the Christmas feast where his parents still kept a vacant chair awaiting his homecoming. Finally, surrounded by his loved ones, he sank exhausted into the chair that had stood unused these 12 years past.

All watched horrified as the chair legs crumbled. throwing Tom backwards to crack his head on the hearthstone. He lay motionless.

"Dead!" cried his dad. "Murdered! By woodworm!"

Sunshine

It was a low sun.

A sun that struck like a blow to the back of the eyes as rays skimmed the top of the hillside horizon. To the farthermost corner of the barn the light searched, stealing in through the carelessly left open door. Like a burglar, like a detective, moving inexorably, examining every corner before the horizon rose to cover the sun and return blackness.

Marjorie, passing the door, looked in to see why it was open. The final finger of sunlight directed her to the far corner.

She stopped.

The newly disturbed earth was unmistakably a grave.

By Richard Wilson

Something had to be done about it

After two glasses of rose, she announced something had to done about it, it could not wait a moment longer.

She reappeared with the cat clippers and set to.

After a few minutes she paused, deciding her glasses would help her get on better.

Duly bespectacled, with the added aid of scissors, she carried on as before.

When all was done, I looked in the mirror.

It was certainly going to make staying at home a bit easier for a while.

Even self-isolation.

The lockdown haircut.

She assured me she had looked up what to do on U-tube.

By Andrew Ayre

Untitled

In the cold bleak times of the day echoes still swirl from the battles of the previous night.

It was magnificent, but not war.

Now we are becalmed, waiting. Unspoilt before the next encounter.

The day decays to night, the boundaries are marked by the waiting. Saxophone. Long rasping tones. Trumpet. Hard echoes. Drums. Repeat, repeat. Bass, bass, bass. Then it starts.

It is hard to hold the line, it takes you one way and then turns without you noticing.

Then you are somewhere else you never knew existed.

Relax.

And then go again.

And again.

By Jim Donnelly

Untitled - Jackson Pollock, 1948

A Winning Yellow Piece of Pie

A Saturday night in 1989. The call of the Brown Bear is strengthening. Friends Raj, Shan and Coosty push to finish their game to answer the call.

Shan and Coosty both have 5 pieces of pie and are marching up to the centre of the board.

Shan arrives first. Raj grins wickedly as he picks up the question card.

History, the thing his mate is most Shan at. He looks at the card, he looks at Shan.

"Which town in the UK is still at war with Russia."

"Bereeek" answers a gobsmacked Shan.

"Aye," replies Coosty. "Drinks on you Raj."

By Denise Bradshaw

The Contributors

ANDREW AYRE, a resident of Tweedmouth, founded the Wilson's Tales Project in 2013 to celebrate and revive interest in Wilson's Tales and some of the local stories and heritage embedded in them.

He first became aware of the Tales as a child, when the title was given to someone to perform as a New Year charade. Now an accountant by profession, he has maintained a keen interest in history, literature and local events. He is currently reading his way through the Tales and researching for future events, publications and talks.

www.wilsonstales.co.uk

ANDREA WILLIAMS divides her time among seemingly random interests. Turning timber into sawdust, with firewood and occasional furniture as a by-product. Writing short stories – some science fiction, some short science fiction. Practising old skills such as breadmaking and dry stone walling.

Resurrecting old artefacts such as pit saws and PC-DOS. "Now that I'm able to look back at mid-life crises from the far side," she says, "Most of life falls into its correct perspective – which is to say that today's pace of life is best viewed from the roadside rather than the driver's seat."

CHRISTINE FLETCHER: I have always remained fairly anonymous in times past, but have contributed to all the Revival Editions so far except Volume 1. I dramatised "The Prisoner of War Tale" for a Paxton House performance, and "Grizel Cochrane's Tale" for a project in Belford regarding the Dissenters of 1685.

DENISE BRADSHAW was born, brought up and educated in Berwick upon Tweed. Lucky enough to have her interest in reading and literature nurtured by Derek Butler when studying English at Berwick High School and has never stopped loving words, stories or language since then. Using the techniques of good story tellers she continue to effectively present case facts and relevant circumstances in her work as a lawyer. Now living in Ipswich and working mainly in the British Indian Ocean she still loves returning home to Berwick to spend time with family, touch base with her roots and regroup.

JAN ANDERSON, retired after 35 years as a Local Government Officer in Northumberland, I'm able now to indulge my passion in family history research, and have traced my family – on both sides – to Norham, near Berwick, in the late 1700's.

Another passion in creative writing has led me to the Wilson's Tales Project though I first came across Tales of the Borders in a musty shop in Richmond, North Yorkshire in the late 1970's. It's good to see my rather tatty copy back in the Borders and the Tales being given new life.

email: Jananderson3000@gmail.com

JIM HERBERT has lived in Berwick for 40 years and worked in the heritage industry for the past 20. He loves the history of Berwick-upon-Tweed, Northumberland and the Borders. As well as being a historian he is a designer, actor, technician and siege engineer!

Jim runs Berwick Time Lines, a service offering, among other things, regular tours and talks. He writes a regular Berwick Time Lines blog. Dedicated to Berwick's rich history, he researches stories of the town, its people and buildings, often discovering new truths about the past. He also loves prog rock and playing pool.

For more information about services and Jim's blog, visit www.berwicktimelines.com and www.berwicktimelines.tumblr.com

JOE LANG began his writing career as a journalist, playwright and advertising copywriter. He started a London-based communications consultancy business, which he ran for 30 years before moving to Berwick and rediscovering the joys of freelance life.

joe@kaineslang.com

KEITH RYAN was born on the right side of the Tweed at Castle Hills Maternity Home and educated at Berwick Grammar School. He is a solicitor by trade, historian by nature, and Lisbon Lion in his dreams. Author of Bloody Berwick, a history of the town when it stood centre stage in three centuries of Anglo-Scottish medieval warfare, he has his boots by his bed for when the call comes from Celtic Park.

keithryan3@aol.com   www.bloodyberwick.com

MICHAEL A. FENTY is a retired GP living in Coldingham. He has been writing for many years – initially articles for medical magazines and later, after retirement, drama.

Michael's play The Resurrection Man – based on the letters and trial documents of local doctor George Laurie, tried in 1820 for grave robbing – was performed by the New Strides Theatre Company; and in 2013 he contributed four short plays to a dramatised walk in the Lammermuirs – The Footsteps of Flodden. In 2016, his play Tibbie Tamson was performed by the Borders Youth Theatre

The Royal Raid and The Monks of Dryburgh were the first two dramatisations for Wilson's Tales. His next, The Monomaniac, was performed at Paxton House in 2014 and can still be seen on youtube with www.youtube.com/watch?v=Yps8-uo8RD4&feature=youtu.b

Michael's blog Gangril Days is at http://gangrildays.blogspot.co.uk/

MICHAEL SCOTT-WATSON was born and bred in the borders, but educated at boarding schools and read Classics at New College, Oxford. After a short spell working for a publisher he came back to the family farm outside Kelso over 20 years ago to become the fifth generation working the land. Although he thinks he may have a novel inside him, all that has come out so far are speeches for birthday parties and weddings, and unpublished poems.

RICHARD WILSON is an aspiring eccentric, whose early love of writing and storytelling was set aside whilst founding software and marketing companies. Yorkshireman by birth and inclination, he claims Northumbrian descent by virtue of the Anglo-Saxon kingdoms boundary starting at the River Humber.

Now back in the home of real ale, real people, and great crack he's using his time to restore furniture, understand and practice old skills and despair of modern technologies and anti social media. Looking back over harrumph years to his pre-internet childhood usually results in comments like "In our day we didn't need facebook, phones, computers, tv or bottled water to run around in harmless gangs annoying people and being given an occasional clatter round t' lugs to keep us in our place."

WTP@Yorkshireman.info

DR TONY DOUGLAS. I first learned of Wilsons Tales at a meeting of the St Boswell's Writing Forum. My cousin Joan was a reporter at the Berwick Advertiser circa 50 years ago. Connecting the two, piqued my interest in assisting the Wilsons tale project Team to retell one of the tales in this edition. It was a joy to do. I have recently completed my first historical fiction novel entitled 'Inextricably Linked'. These activities have opened up, quite literally, a new chapter in my life!